Hard Luck
& Heavy Rain

Hard Luck
& Heavy Rain

The Ecology of Stories
in Southeast Texas

JOSEPH C. RUSSO

DUKE UNIVERSITY PRESS　DURHAM AND LONDON　2023

Designed by MaTThew Tauch
Typeset in Arno Pro and Alegreya Sans
by Westchester Publishing Services

Library of Congress Cataloging-in-Publication Data
Names: Russo, Joseph C., [date] author.
Title: Hard luck and heavy rain : the ecology of stories in Southeast
Texas / Joseph C. Russo.
Description: Durham : Duke University Press, 2022. | Includes
bibliographical references and index.
Identifiers: LCCN 2022027008 (print)
LCCN 2022027009 (ebook)
ISBN 9781478019053 (paperback)
ISBN 9781478016410 (hardcover)
ISBN 9781478023685 (ebook)
Subjects: LCSH: Ethnology—Texas. | Country life—Texas. | Sexual
minorities—Texas. | Texas—Social life and customs. | Texas—
Civilization. | Texas—Social conditions. | BISAC: SOCIAL SCIENCE /
Anthropology / Cultural & Social | SOCIAL SCIENCE / LGBTQ
Studies / General
Classification: LCC F391.2 .R877 2022 (print) | LCC F391.2 (ebook) |
DDC 305.8009764—dc23/eng/20220816
LC record available at hTTps://lccn.loc.gov/2022027008
LC ebook record available at hTTps://lccn.loc.gov/2022027009

Chapter 3 photo courtesy of the author. Cover and all other
interior photos by Miles Baldi.

for Deb

There are parts of Texas where a fly lives ten thousand years and a man can't die soon enough. Time gets strange there from too much sky, too many miles from crack to crease in the flat surface of the land.

KATHERINE DUNN, *GEEK LOVE*

Contents

Acknowledgments

This book has been about five years in the making, gathering around it all sorts of people on its journey to the shelf. Some observed from outside, scratching their heads in bewilderment. Some pored over its every detail and found things that even I didn't see. Some wandered into its composition, a few without even meaning to—I hope that they feel the love that I felt for them when I put their stories down. I hope that whoever finds themselves turning the pages of this book does so forgivingly, remembering I was just another character here.

I want to thank my good friends in the anthropology PhD program and elsewhere at the University of Texas, Austin. They were the first to listen to what I was thinking and commented on my ideas graciously: Danielle Good, Julie Conquest, Ana Isabel Fernández de Alba, Alejandro M. Flores Aguilar, Juan Pablo González, Anthony Dest, Daniel Pereira, Aniruddhan Vasudevan, and Nóra Tyeklár. I'd also like to acknowledge the time and generosity of the faculty members who served as valuable mentors: Kathleen Stewart, Marina Peterson, Craig Campbell, Courtney Handman, and Ann Cvetkovich. Their suggestions made this book better.

My colleagues and students at Purchase College and Wesleyan University have provided me with the space to flourish and grow as a nontraditional scholar and teacher, a space I never thought I'd find out in the world. I am grateful for their unconditional support and inspiration in these precarious times. Thanks so much to Shaka McGlotten, Jason Pine, Lorraine Plourde, David Kim, Rudi Gaudio, Daniella Gandolfo, Betsy Traube, Margot Weiss, Anu Sharma, and Joey Weiss.

My doctoral adviser Katie Stewart saved my life in 2013, after a near fatal encounter with British academia. I can't express in words what she has done for me, how much her guidance and friendship have touched me. She is the sort of mentor who makes you listen to yourself, guides you gently, and doesn't try to mold you into another version of themselves. I'll never forget her telling our awestruck class of nervous grad students to make our work capacious, not just a straight line but "something to walk around." When I was having a crisis in the field in 2015, I called her from my little travel trailer on the edge of Beaumont, Texas, and she told me to expand the scope of my vision, to "write it all." I did just that, and the result is this book.

This work would not have been possible without the support of an ACLS/Mellon Dissertation Completion Fellowship, for which I am grateful.

Thanks to my amazing editors at Duke University Press, Ken Wissoker and Josh Gutterman Tranen, and the generous comments of two stellar anonymous readers. Thanks also to the copyediting skills and careful eye of my friend Ben Gross.

Thank you to Miles Baldi, who accompanied me on a road trip to Southeast Texas in the summer of 2021 in order to realize my visions for the book's artwork. His photos grace the pages and make the book feel more real and more special.

Thank you to my friends and family, especially my mother, Toni Russo, for sticking it out with me all these years and always seeing something worth encouraging in me.

Special thanks to the dynastic families of Southeast Texas who let me poke around in their lives for a decade or so without too much complaint. The names have been changed, but the stories remain the same. Thanks most of all to my best friend, Danny Lane Russell of Vidor, Texas, who brought me to a place but showed me a world.

Introduction

Falling into the Big Thicket

All hidden kingdoms have their thresholds. Entering Southeast (SE) Texas from Houston, you cross the Old and Lost Rivers. Great egrets, vast white sheets, fly low over the Interstate 10 bridge that spans these tributaries. In long-distance flying, egrets and herons hold their legs straight out behind them, but in their leaps over the bridge, their stilt legs dangle downward in a game of chance with eighteen-wheelers careening past. I have seen the feet of egrets brush the tops of trucks.

It is as if the birds are initiating travelers eastward in the growing proximity to SE Texas and its Big Thicket, the "biological crossroads of North America"[1]—that great tangle of piney woods, swamp, church, and smoke. Past the bridge, the land gets flat and low. You cross the main river from which the Old and Lost diverge: the Trinity River, what many SE Texans identify as the real border between SE Texas and the rest of the state. It references the Catholic Holy Trinity, of course, but I always thought of the trinity of Texan industry: the Golden Triangle of Beaumont, Port Arthur, and Orange.[2] Southern turnoffs lead to the coastal marshes and prairies of Anahuac that give way to Galveston Bay, where ibises and spoonbills, with their carotenoid-pigmented red eyes, preen in the cattails, and brown pelicans fly in a ponderous single file along the coastline in perfect unison, slow to flap or change altitude. There is an ancient time to the procession of these heavy, antediluvian birds, who hurl themselves into the ocean with such force that it seems they have broken their wings upon the waves. A moment later they float to the surface with fish in their throat pouches, harried by gulls.

Slowly, oil refineries begin to mar the vistas east. At night this is a striking vision, a refinery lit and throbbing like a brilliant city—the force of its output casting a haze above it that blurs the stars in the night sky. Fire belching from the flares gives it the appearance of a fort, a gated forge. Near the fence, you can feel the whole complex pulsate. But it is rare to see a person standing in such an interstice, as the highway is a breakneck thoroughfare, loose truck tire treading sloughed off on the road like the skin of giant snakes. A human walking along the shoulder of the interstate is a signal of something askew, and the rare ones in flip flops, or full camping gear, or sometimes bare-chested with nothing but basketball shorts and a can of something in a paper bag, seem to be on long walks to nowhere.

The road's shoulder is a repository of detritus; the roadkill of the American interstate is particularly distressed, unrecognizable clumps of meat, entrails dramatically strewn about by the omniscient vultures that maintain an air of absolute apathy amid dangerous speed and fiery sky. Or deer contorted beyond possibility: you can see the face of that icon, the trucker, reflected in his dashboard screen, thrown into a frenzy of paranoia from weak truck stop coffee and an overload of CB slang, bearing down upon the unfortunate beasts whose last moment was entrapment between a median wall and a tire. It is difficult to imagine some pleasure wasn't taken in creating such elaborate carnage. Or maybe in the deep routine of his path along the interstate, nothing that stands in the way registers for him, the speed fixation takes over. Just a zooming canister of goods; at night they whoosh past you in a rhythm. The flatness of the road takes you in. Finally the trance is broken by Big Beau, a gargantuan alligator made of metal siding and rubber and painted in a garish green,[3] welcoming you with jaws agape into Beaumont. You have reached Gator Country Adventure Park, home of Big Tex, the largest live-captured "nuisance alligator" in the United States at thirteen feet, eight inches. The scene of the road east is replete with such visions.

The Ecology of Stories

This book traces what I call an ecology, inhabited by stories, characters, and places.[4] The stories fall under the loose umbrella of hard-luck stories, though not all of them relate experiences of hardship. I see stories as narrative events that do more than tell: they experiment, they play, and they perform the world that they are in.[5] The stories convey feelings that position the teller as having been through something that stays with them: *this is how I got here, and this is how it stuck to me.* In this sense, stories are what Derek P. McCormack calls "shaped forms that proposition us as discrete presences while also drawing attention to the clouds of affective and material relations in which they are generatively immersed."[6] The hard-luck stories of the folks whom I dwelt among in SE Texas's Golden Triangle are a reminder of what many Americans, Texans among them, see the whole region as a repository for: *the accrual of bad feeling.*

The hard-luck form is a genre of story told through a mode of framing that I identify within the regional form of Texan storytelling. To trace hard luck is to follow the tension that is created when new stories come from an "old" place. It is to hear the great impasse that this region finds itself at with the "outside" and to hear the stories that are generated that make sense of this profound impingement. The scene of the impasse, what Lauren Berlant has defined as "a space of time lived without a narrative genre," foregrounds the comportment of hard-luck stories, making them at times frustratingly textured objects.[7] Hard-luck stories trace the movement and resonance in the void left by life without a genre—the persisting of time and voice in the space of stuckness. At once presenting a set of qualities, a style of speech, recurrent themes—belonging to a default void genre or genre of stultification—these stories function to ring out in the impasse, to untether the speaker and the listener from a direction that might make sense for them to travel toward. So they are of a genre composed of vibrant qualities within a place that I thought of as the waiting room of what to do next while listening to the accounts of the people I met in the cities and towns of SE Texas. They express a stuckness, a suspension of action. Story after story is prefaced with how nothing is happening here, but told with the vibrant repertoire of feelings and utterances of this place as a locus of action. The impasse manifests ethnographically through this theme; there is a conceptual arrest at play, the great mythological stagnancy of the American South and its inhabitants that is deployed as a rhetorical device lamenting the backward, the ignorant, and the archaic remnants of American feeling. The hard-luck stories zoom in to focus on being stuck in one's life as a mode.

A story's texture crafts a way out of the banal fantasy of the bad place, exceeding the dyad of good or bad. This type of story is not peculiar to SE Texas, but it is produced here with a persistent intensity. I was never without stories in SE Texas, whether I wanted them or not, and whether they made sense to me or not. The SE Texan public depicted here, who by no means constitute an ideologically unified group, are not presupposed as occupying a rung on a social hierarchy. Their position is not beholden to power structures alone: here, they are "not only" the rural whites of the liberal imaginary.[8] They are not only the pitiable, marginalized, and ideologically brainwashed of this imaginary, a fulcrum for liberal forms of political fantasy. In an exploratory spirit, this ethnographic practice seeks to exceed the limit of what such a public has come to signify by attuning to stories that take us into the space of excess itself.[9]

The question of character is taken up as a heuristic within the discipline of anthropology and elsewhere. Walter Benjamin, in his 1931 manifesto "The Destructive Character," speaks of a critical object at once personified and abstracted that seems to lie somewhere between specificity and generality. He tries to wrest the meaning of character away from its modern context within psychoanalysis and morality by using it to describe a somewhat mythological typology: figures in an atmosphere, recognizable to all, yet unquantifiable by any reasonable method. Anthropology, and its notorious post–World War II "national character studies" conducted by luminaries like Ruth Benedict and Margaret Mead, drew ire in the following years for their base generalizations about common personality traits of whole cultures and their flattened images of those cultures in the form of ethnic stereotypes.[10] More recently, anthropologists have explored the question of character in its relation to religion and ethics.[11] The way I speak of character in this book explores some of these paths, but it is primarily taken from the very ordinary way character is used in the conversations I had both in SE Texas and throughout my lifetime, just hearing people tell stories and speak about characters. Over and over again, folks I spoke to in SE Texas would discover that I was "collecting stories" and refer me to people by saying, "You should speak to X. They're a real character."

"The Texan" has become an emergent character, more than just a person who can be found dwelling in the world. The Texan character is close to a figuration, something like a catalog of archetypes.[12] I sometimes think of the playing out of the closed story of America as an automated mimetic process of anthropomorphizing a place, in the sense of picturing cartoon human avatars when we think of the qualities of a locale.[13] We envision a map with figures standing within the borders of each state, each nation, like the mascots of sports teams. I see character as a concept that sits uncomfortably between the underlying tensions of the ethnographic method: the fruitful impossibility in the pull between comparativist and particularist approaches to analysis.[14] These characters shift, they are subject to the temporal, the local, the racialized—they persist despite being temporary, of their time, things that pass.

The threshold into the kingdom of SE Texas, across the Old and Lost Rivers, marks the entrance to an "old and lost" place in American social imaginaries. Old and lost speak as much to the remoteness of the region as they do to a catalog of feelings, the feelings of a place of old and lost ways. Once you're deep in the undergrowth, what locals call the "tight-eye," where the thicket is so dense that SE Texans say a rattlesnake has to back out of it, the accrual of these feelings can be claustrophobic. This threshold is more than the moment you enter the obscured zone of SE Texas. Despite the fact that the look of the land changes from hilly to flat and piney as you enter it from the west, and that the voting map goes from blue to red as you leave Houston for the country, this is not just the ecological or political gateway to the Deep South. It is a gateway into a circulation of feeling, where the hard-luck stories ring out from its spaces.

The ecologies of SE Texas can be observed in dazzling variation, owing to the disparate array of ecosystems that occur across a relatively concentrated region. The place that later became Texas, inhabited and hazardously traversed by the Panther Band of the Western Atakapa, was a wondrously varied catalog of ecosystems.[15] Later, French and Spanish explorers and Appalachian settlers, as well as escaped slaves, convicts, and deserting soldiers, arrived to carve out paths that became roads and make hideouts that became hidden villages. As the rise of the great Texan industries, lumber and oil, transformed the land, these ecosystems encountered new entanglements with other impingements: piney woods razed of longleaf pine and infested with pine beetles, and Gulf Coast beaches blackened with oil.[16] The historical account is that place gave way to the dream of an "America out there," what Alexis de Tocqueville saw as an almost mystical migration West that brought Americans into a wanderlust tethered to promise, "mystics of materialism, caught up in a contagious mass movement, a *völkerwanderung* fueled by the romantic prose that gushed forth from the pens of the Western propagandizers."[17] This is the SE Texan ecology that you encounter today; it is the ongoing composition of place where the materialist-speculative boom-or-bust economy festers, and the intensity of these fluctuating conditions produce severe forms of life. The place where the promises of the gushing prose of speculation manifested on January 10, 1901, straight from the bowels of the earth: oil.

The swamps and baygall are not only filled with fascinating flora and fauna—they are also filled with the hauntings of stories. Like the campfire tales of the Dog People, who hid whiskey stills in the thicket and roved the land with their packs of curs, carving out a living in the Neches River Bottom.[18] The ethnic and racial histories of the region are entangled, too, in an often-tense blend of Cajun-Louisiana and Anglo-Texan cultures, of vivid Black American and Creole diasporas and rigidly anti-Black, white supremacist hotbeds.[19] SE Texas is a meeting-place of debauchery and conservatism, of the queer body and its assailants—often occurring in the same subjects, in the same stories. It is the crossroads of deep funda-mentalism and profound sins. There is something extra in its regionality—what one Texas travel website cheekily calls a *lagniappe*, from the Loui-siana French term (adopted from Quechua) for a bonus thrown into a transaction by a merchant.[20]

Whiteness, Badness, Stuckness

I write this in 2021 with some ambivalence. The past four years of Donald Trump's America seem to have redefined the lines of politics along fairly clear identity boundaries; once again, people are speaking, without any hesitation, of "us and them." This happens everywhere, in all the places that I have known, during moments when categories are thrown into crisis, as I feel they have been in the United States. I see these reestablished bound-aries as a kind of projection, especially with regard to whiteness. There is an anxiety to align or disidentify with the various strands of whiteness that emerge, to absolve oneself of the responsibility of being associated with the "source of the trouble," whatever that is. So it is that the nature of these ambiguous and evasive boundaries, how they are constituted and what they are composed of, take different forms.

Whenever I have shared my work at an academic conference or even in more casual situations among friends, I am often met with the ques-tion, "Why would you want to do research there, on such people?" The implication is that I am wasting time by spending time among "them," that whatever situations I find myself in "there" are somehow not worth the trouble of being among them. "Them," in this instance, refers to "bad whites"—a composite category that includes a wide swath of qualities. The most recent shorthand for bad whites is "Trump supporters." What is being presupposed is twofold. First, the coherence of a "them" category is assumed, a population of millions, a hivemind of terrible beliefs inhabiting a defined geographical zone of pollution. Second, the coherence of an "us" category assumes the unmarked space of the rational speaker. This rationality takes many forms: secular, liberal, humanist—but also educated, kind, future-oriented. This has always been something that gives me pause in my thinking around SE Texas as a fieldsite, and SE Texans as figures who complicate the ethnographic encounter. Anthropology, and the way anthropologists speak about the value of what we do, is based in part around the exploration and writing of difference as a benign and valuable framework. But I found in these discussions with colleagues and friends that white SE Texans are bad whites: people for whom benign difference is disallowed by virtue of their uncomfortable proximity to white rational liberalism in the United States. They are not the didactic ethnographic object of anthropology; anything to be learned from them is presupposed as a bad idea, soiled knowledge, closure.

There seems to be no established route into comfortably relativizing the ways of those who stand as the roadblock to good liberalism. Bad whites are not distanced Others, but *near-Others*, figures whose resistance to the gestures of dismissal trouble the unmarked category of rationality.[21] These are Others whose existence abrades against "our" attachments to whiteness, nationality, and regionalism. They expose the limits of this distancing of the unmarked category by creating a discomfort in the ethnographer-informant relation. Having already upended the distance of the Other by focusing on those who are not only "at home with us" but also not enshrouded in the academic use of the category of indigeneity because of their position as the descendants of the settlers, disenfranchised and antagonistic, the usual approaches to the Other are short-circuited.[22] There is no way we can familiarize otherness without admitting the Other into our space—which of course they already inhabit.

The feeling of SE Texas acted on me, undoubtedly, and I couldn't help but allow the intensity of this feeling to shape the way that I listened and the way that I wrote. The hard-luck stories shared here are not followed by decoding processes in which I tell the reader what the storyteller means in relation to the bigger picture. Sometimes to sit in the story is to be wrapped into its telling. The feeling of this kingdom can be forbidding: it is the exhaustive (and exhausted) list of industry's excesses, of anti-Black terror, of remote and feral rurality. A composition of America's shadowy scenes, the kinds that even Texans from other places raise their eyebrows upon hearing. Whenever the SE Texan town of Vidor is mentioned, something instantly comes to mind. People remember a Confederate flag flying from a local high school, stories of people dying of cancers beneath the plumes of refinery smoke, stories about Black mothers warning their kids not to stop for gas in the "sundown towns," where, according to many, a sign on the highway that threatened Black people to stay out of Vidor after dark was on display until the early 1980s.[23] The threshold is not a definitive line over which the place or the people comprise some otherness—but to think of it as a crossing-over is to give space to difference, and to the feeling of difference. To give space to the perspicacity of a region in knowing and performing the repertoire of its notorieties that complicate assumed simplicity, and sometimes throw those simplicities back into your face amplified, as if to say: "What you heard about me is true—and that isn't even the half of it."[24]

A deep frame of this work addresses the lamentation of "what is to be done" given that the contemporary political atmosphere of the United States has reached an unprecedented impasse. This impasse should not altogether be thought of as new. Benjamin's historical theses conceived of history as an accumulation of ruins.[25] Paul Klee's *Angelus Novus*, Benjamin's "angel of history," seems to be caught now in a precipice between reaching toward messianic time and the truism, uttered with a shrug and a long drag on a cigarette, that "history repeats itself." The political atmosphere is simultaneously new and old, and ways of attuning to this paradox run the gamut from lamentation to cynicism. History is not over, and people are roaming around in the pleasure and pain of its forming.[26] I encountered people who seemed stuck in this roaming, which made me think about the historical present as an impasse that, despite ostensibly describing a lack of movement forward, still has things to tell us: impasses are not voids—they have messy contents that convey signals. It might be the effects of these contents that flounder in an endpoint of stuckness.

What the impasse conveys is that the "the way things are now" is a fruition of bad feelings, what the media has pointed out with some shock as the arsenal of Trump's rural white working class, his "emboldened" masses. The danger of seeing the actions of these masses as new is not only myopic in the immediate sense of forgetting the cyclical nature of reactionary political moments in the United States. It also does not take into account the strange temporality of Benjamin's version of history, which tells us that while the quirks of the impasse may be new, while Trump's rhetorical strategies may be novel, the elements underneath them are not. Beside the fact that the rural white working class was not solely responsible for the election of Trump, it is vital to pay attention to how such an image, possibly even a specter, of rural whiteness is raised to not only purify oneself and one's immediate context from the source of bad feeling, but to identify the places where the bad, dangerous people are and to bolster a great American story: the story of the feral whites out in the badlands, stuck in time, gnashing their teeth and waiting to strike.

Most people I knew in SE Texas felt that America was stuck, and for them, the stuckness was most deeply felt in their economically depressed, forgotten region. But in many ways, SE Texas is a paradox, an example of what Kim Fortun might call a thriving late industrial zone where the burgeoning, inestimable wealth of the petrochemical industry and its minority of benefactors acts as a smokescreen to obscure the suffering of the masses.[27] It is also true that the majority of Texans voted for Trump in hopes of alleviating this impasse.[28] Many of the expressed viewpoints with regard to race, religion, gender, and sexuality, which would be considered repugnant by most liberals, had direct connections to the alleviation of this impasse. Various hierarchies, in which they found themselves at the bottom, were destroying their lives. There was a pervasive idea that people of color, LGBTQ+ people, minorities of every kind were doing better than they were because of "government handouts" and other conspiracies. I heard these opinions expressed not only by white men, but by women, people of color, and LGBTQ+ people—the very people these unfounded claims were leveled against, apparently turning the weapon against themselves. But also, these so-called minorities were speaking from a position of exception justified by what I came to understand as a stubbornly Texan individualism: *I ain't like them.* Some of them, in short, lived up to the stereotypes in the way they spoke and what they thought. And then others didn't.

The impasse is not just stuckness, but a set of encounters that its inhabitants experience. Styling themselves along a spectrum of types, from witty observer to scarred warrior, storytellers not only voice the recognizable ideology of Trump's America—they display the somatic attunements of daily life in a region conceived broadly as a sacrifice zone, a place where the negative elements of the way things are now have come home to roost.[29] There are expressive elements to these stories that contextualize how a nonpolitician with a Weberian charismatic appeal could grab the attention of such a public, capitalizing on the excesses and affects of a region characterized by the story of being stuck. The excesses preceded Trump and will linger long after the broken promises, which have already begun to sting, fade away.

In this book, the frame of ecology is more than biological, more than physically environmental. I follow the lines of social ecology drawn by thinkers such as Gregory Bateson, Félix Guattari, and Murray Bookchin, who maintain that the ecological conditions of life are deeply interwoven with sociality. It is not my contention that bad people make a bad planet, or vice versa. Rather, what I learned from talking to the folks in SE Texas was that in the state of impending eco-collapse that we find ourselves in and that we have brought ourselves up to the precipice of meeting, life flickers on in intense ways. I trace what it feels like to be in a place at the heart of the impasse at multiple levels: economic, environmental, semiotic. When I drive back into SE Texas, I think of it as entering "the Zone," an idea I first encountered in the 1979 Andrei Tarkovsky film *Stalker*. The film describes an isolated, difficult to access area of a world that operates by some unknown and dire logic. And it presents to its unfortunate visitors an eco-portrait of place at its most harmed, mutated. In the Zone, time operates differently and the prospect of getting out of it once you enter feels impossible.

Aftereffects

After I left SE Texas for the last time in 2016, a number of world-shifting developments took place. The first was, of course, the election of Trump, which occurred only a few months after I left. I had watched the momentum of the election building up over the course of my fieldwork and the many visits I had made to SE Texas prior to that time. The element of Trump was introduced in a more significant way as the election date approached. On return visits, I noticed people clinging tenaciously to the idea of Trump. He had squashed the other candidates, and it looked as though there was no choice but to respect that sort of steamrolling—besides, he made superficial concessions to the working people. I noticed that these mentions were read as winks, almost conspiratorial in nature, to working-class whites. But even beyond that, Trump's comments about "helping the workers" were read as messages to white people, many of them middle and upper class, who somehow identified with or valorized the poetic idea of the disenfranchised, decentered American white working person. The intensities of this resultant atmosphere created a host of new scenes that people found themselves in, ranging across the spectrum of hope, denial, newly sparked rage, or a deeper and more impenetrable hopelessness.

The second event was Hurricane Harvey in the late summer of 2017, which completely engulfed SE Texas and affected many of the sites that I had lived in, including the RV park in Beaumont and nearby Vidor. It was a reminder of the perpetuity of hurricane disasters in SE Texas, and the immediate media reaction to the event marked it once again as a symbolic sticking point. I watched a wave of studied apathy on social media, relegating those who were suffering to the flattened category of climate change deniers. On the other side, inspirational stories of communities "coming together" in the face of the hurricane offered a counterpoint. People waded through the floodwaters, rescued on boats by local volunteer groups like the Cajun Navy, their lives washed away like so much detritus in the storm.[30]

The third was COVID-19, in 2020. The landlord of a trailer park, one of my key informants in this book, contracted the virus and was briefly intubated before being flown to a hospital in Houston where he received further treatment and recovered. I stayed in contact with him intermittently during the ordeal. He caught the virus at a party, before there was any uniform messaging in the United States about social distancing or masks (made more complicated by Texas government officials' generally lax and even nihilistic attitude toward the virus in general), and texted me long supplications to please be safe and to "take this thing seriously."[31] The tone of his messages warning me about "Corona 19" surprised me, because many of my informants whom I had stayed in touch with after leaving the field didn't believe COVID was real. In fact, since 2017, I had noticed a lot of their ways of thinking and the stories explored in this book had further mutated into what can only be called "conspiracist thinking." Many of them, especially the ladies in the health food store (chapter 2), had already been onboard with these strands of thought. They ranged from anti-vaxxers, to believing that certain dead celebrities or politicians were still alive and that certain living politicians were dead, to having histories in militias and millenarian movements. The Trump presidency and the birth of the urconspiracy movement called QAnon seemed to both intensify and focus these beliefs into a shared mode, and it also spread these beliefs beyond the traditional confines of where we find conspiracy thinking.

QAnon is a pro-Trump, quasi-secular millenarian movement that began online in October 2017 when a mysterious user called "Q" (short for Q Clearance Patriot) posted a series of cryptic, instructional warnings to "patriots" on the notoriously right-wing imageboard website 4chan.[32] QAnon has seeped into the collective consciousness and real-life events (such as the January 6, 2021, storming of the US Capitol), foreseeing an era of societal unrest called "The Storm" that draws on multiple previous conspiracy theories in a collection of beliefs that can be traced back to the early twentieth century.[33]

QAnon is composed of a dazzling pastiche of narratives that center around the idea that Donald Trump is battling a deep state run by a Satanic pedophilic cabal whose members drink the adrenochrome-rich blood of children and clandestinely rule the world, hiding in plain sight. From this baseline allegation, hundreds of conspiracy theories reveling in the spectacular mythos of what Susan Lepselter calls the "American Uncanny" proliferate across epochs and cultures.[34] They capture major US politicians and celebrities in their tendrils and blast populist dogma through Q drops, apocryphal messaging uploaded periodically to a website, Qmap, with more than 10 million monthly users.[35] Qmap served as QAnon's sacred palimpsest until it was shut down in September 2020.

After I left SE Texas, I stayed in touch with many of my informants and friends via text and email. I noticed that Q talk had seeped into all kinds of ideas about history, politics, religion, health, and culture. It was a new and exciting narrative for people who were still looking for a way out of the feeling of stuckness, but it was largely composed of a collage of old ideas and paranoias. In retrospect, I see the conversations and stories in this book as the documentation of a prescient or anticipatory moment: right before the shift into millions of Americans waiting for Trump to unleash The Storm and bring about The Great Awakening.

Getting Into Things

When I first came to SE Texas in the summer of 2008, it was for a funeral. My best friend Danny's grandmother had died, his Meemaw. The service was held in the main room of a funeral home in his hometown of Vidor. The room was new-feeling and beige carpeted, with shiny pews and artificial flowers. It felt like a room where you might have day camp on a rainy day or an AA meeting. Meemaw was laid out in her closed casket, and a line of people, mostly old-timers, queued up to pay their respects. It was a new experience for me, having grown up Catholic in the northeast in the world of open-casket wakes and morose cemetery rituals. It fell somewhere between my understanding of a wake and a funeral—a Southern Baptist "service." The pastor was coiffed, jovial. He talked about what a good, godly lady Meemaw had been and how he knew her husband personally—they even played golf together. It seemed clear that he hadn't actually known her, and that this was somehow beside the point. A screen lowered from the ceiling with a loud, mechanical drone, and images of Meemaw and her family were projected on it. Music played over the speakers—Christian easy listening, devotional hymns. The air conditioning billowed the screen slightly, warping the images.

Afterward, the whole family gathered in the gravel parking lot under the glaring Texas summer sun. They are a dynastic working-class family in the Texas style, ten siblings, gatherings full of laughter and tears, hard-luck yarns, deep feuds that carry on for years where guns are drawn in driveways over financial matters, infidelities, or the unhinged moment of a person driven to the edge. Betrayals, alliances, dark rumors, absurdity, the swirling about of an excessive atmosphere. They adopted me without hesitation on that first visit, initiating me with ribald humor and quasi-accusatory indictments. A libertarian uncle of Danny's demanded to know why "you New Yorkers make us wear seatbelts!," which I was never really able to answer. Underneath this ritualized induction, I could tell they appreciated the way I rolled with the punches. They joked about how brave a Yankee was to "come all the way up here," even though I had come down—way, way down. They are the reason this book exists; their stories breathe life into the atmosphere of the place. They showed patience when I continually prodded them to retell stories, to be recorded, to consider elements of the things they were saying so that I could "bring all this stuff back to Austin where y'all are gonna laugh at us!," as Deb, Danny's mom, used to suggest, only half-joking. Their love and their loyalty haunt me, and it isn't without a bit of shame that I share this clumsy glimpse into their world, hoping to be more than another element wrapped into their long genealogy of the Bad Things That Happened to Us.

In the decade following that first visit, I learned much about the world that they generously shared with me, sometimes in stories and lessons, and sometimes in inscrutable gestures. I spent countless hours *visitin' with* them, a Southern phrase for hanging out, but one that connotes more profound reciprocity in conversation and active listening. It's time spent slowly, perhaps strangely, with great big pauses that let the stories come as they will. *Visitin' with* correlates to the "deep hanging out" of ethnography, and it was in this mode that I heard the epochs of their lives, sometimes unwittingly.[36] I have seen them love, suffer, move away, get stuck, and leave this earth in an equal measure of unthinkable severity and the easy, gentle way in which you can lean back, turn on the radio, and zone out driving down those long, flat SE Texas highways.

One of Danny's aunts suffered from a rare condition called Moyamoya disease—it constricted arteries in her brain and caused her to have what the doctors called "mini-strokes," resulting in severe cognitive and motor disability. Her family described her as having the "affect" of a child. She was mostly silent but said a few words here and there. During a lull in the conversation in the parking lot after Meemaw's funeral, she slowly lifted her arm and pointed at a spot on the gravel. "Ah see a thang," she said. We asked her what she saw; she kept pointing to a spot in the middle distance. "Ah see a thang." Finally, I recognized a piece of confetti in the gravel. It was barely perceptible—it gave off tiny metallic flickers. "Is that what you see, Brenda Sue?" asked her husband. She didn't answer, kept her hand pointed out: "Ah see a thang."

I was struck by her perceptions of the place she was living in, floating just below the register of talk and so-called normative sociality, but also observant of things that floated just under "our" perception, the attunements of that same field of observation. One of the first questions I asked myself when it became clear to me that I would be doing a project on SE Texas was, What is a thing here? Like Aunt Brenda, I wanted to *visit with* the things just beneath the surface of the obvious that mattered to people. I wanted to listen to the thing being told, and watch the way that told thing joined together with others and flickered into an existence, here enacted by those whose specialty it is to be a character, relatable yet specific, and to enliven these stories with intensities.

One.

The Strange Time of Hard-Luck Stories

Morning Coffee

Morning coffee at the RV park in Beaumont, Texas, was a delicate ritual. It was at once the display of mastery of a storytelling form and a reestablishing of boundaries. What could and could not be admitted into this space was anyone's guess. Yet once the rules were settled on in an improvisatory moment, they were retroactively configured as well established. When the tension broke around a story that might be drifting toward the unsayable, and hoarse laughter spread around the circle of the mostly middle-aged Texan women, then the ordinary settled down again on its comfortable haunches, the field rested, and the next teller readied herself for the trial-by-story. Some failed, and experienced an unofficial banishment from the daily arrangement of camp chairs outside Miss Tina's trailer.

I had been at the RV park for three weeks before they finally asked me what I was doing there among them, these women who had perfected the telling of hard-luck stories, perfected the method of the pregnant pause, the clucking of the tongue, the knowing, sidelong glance, the multifaceted use of "bless your heart," the limits of how far one may delve into the implications of another's story without stirring discomfort, or the stylistic flair of expressive lying—in short, the catalog of modes of talk that comprised the ordinary there.[1] When I told them that I was an ethnographer researching, in part, queer life in SE Texas—a region legendarily hostile to the queer and the non-white, one of the least-educated Metropolitan Statistical Areas in the country and the holder of one of the highest murder rates in the state[2]—they became silent, staring down into their coffees, nervously fiddling with the sequined collars of their Malteses. The smoke of their Virginia Slims hung in the stifling morning humidity, the swamp air. I braced myself for I didn't know what. I felt that I had betrayed the terms of an unspoken contract, that I would be characterized afterward as an aberrant hiccup in the seamlessness of the RV park. *Bless his heart—he didn't tell good stories.* But how profoundly I had misjudged them, the seamlessness of their craft.

The awkward silence, in some miracle of shared atmosphere, shifted into a dramatic double beat. The talk turned exuberantly toward tragicomedies of eccentric queer characters, sprinkled with dark laughter in the remembrance of odd childhood friends: beautiful brilliant brothers lost to Yankee cities or AIDS, old schoolmarms in slacks with rough hands, fey antiques dealers who wore monocles, ebullient choir leaders like Roderick Ferguson's sissies at the picnic, a pantheon of Texan queers wrapped in the pall of loneliness rurality brings.[3] The ordinary expanded into an encounter; a pocket opened in which to accommodate this shift in the object of the hard-luck stories. Instead of cataloging their ailments or reposing in silences around the gravity of the hurricane that destroyed the region, the women's hard-luck stories of the queer character, accursed in its traveling through this ecology, took form.

There were a few days in the RV park when the old-timers didn't come out for morning coffee on account of the heat. Miss Linda, one of the park's elders, peeked out of her Holiday Rambler, deemed it "hot enough to stop a clock," and retreated back into the hum of Fox News. And at that moment nothing seemed truer. Texas summer is time standing still—the refusal of the passing of the hours when nothing holds back the sun as it stands gaping in the sky, and August knocks you clean over if you stumble out of the cool of the air conditioning. Minutes are incinerated. It's the lamentation of a chain gang in a never-ending march down a rural highway, a Terrence Malick haze, a vast scorched expanse. And the Golden Triangle is the sodden, flat pocket of that heat. Locals called it the armpit—nestled down below sea level between the Gulf Coast and Louisiana, dankly humid. The dead must be buried in caskets sealed in cement for fear of washing up in floods. No basements. The rains come violently and wash everything away, leaving a stink in the mist.

When I first arrived at the little RV park, wedged between Beaumont proper and the old rice fields on the way out to Fannett, in the summer of 2015, there was trepidation in the air.[4] There was a surety to the Ted Cruz signs in the little yards next to the lawn flamingos that told me something before I asked. It wasn't just a feeling of trespassing. It was an almost accusatory spark that told me I wasn't paying the proper attention. But Miss Tina was magnanimous and wouldn't take no; she waved me over to hang out with her as soon as she saw me, after the morning coffee klatch had dispersed. Miss Tina was from nearby Vidor, a place "not many folks would wanna go—but it isn't all bad like it *was*." She was a three-time divorcee, smoked Virginia Slims Superslims or Capris. She had been a cheerleader at Vidor High in her youth and remembered a home football game against Thomas Jefferson, a majority-Black high school from nearby Port Arthur, the maligned hometown of Janis Joplin, which featured the hurricane-devastated Pleasure Island. Pleasure Island is a strip of land created by the US Corps of Engineers with dredge deposits left over from creating the Port Arthur Canal in 1899. During the boomtown days and into the 1940s, it featured boardwalks, arcades, ballrooms, and the largest roller coaster in the American South.

The Ku Klux Klan showed up at that football game at Vidor High and burned a cross in the practice field, and Miss Tina thought back to how she had cried. "How terrified those people must have been. This was the early '70s." She had a Maltese named Lacey. Before I left, I asked her whether they had morning coffee there, sitting around her Prowler travel trailer, every day. She said, "Well, it depends on which way the wind's blowin.'" I mistakenly took her to mean that it was a matter of chance, not realizing that in the shadow of the Goodyear plant just down the road in Fannett there were days when the mist came in or the flares were on too high in Nederland and everybody was advised to stay in their trailers. It really *did* depend on the wind.

At morning coffee, folks talked about America needing a dose of Christianity to make things right. One woman joked about her church's sign that Sunday. It asked: "Need a faith lift?" Godlessness was a recurring shadow over morning coffee; the country was sick with it, most thought. And if anyone disagreed, they were met with a smile and a *bless your heart*, the Texan lady's way of telling you that you are beyond the pale. Some of the morning coffee folks were not churchgoers. Their faith was their own, it was private, and they were careful not to ask you about yours either. The mood would shift again, to more rehearsed topics, such as cooking or television or what a nuisance the South Texas State Fair would be when it arrived at Ford Park just up the freeway. You had to make sure to lock your cars and trailers, then—there'd be all sorts of people wandering around. On most mornings, a moment would come when the mood became reminiscent, someone would mention how, back in the 1950s, they used to serve an ice-cream substitute at the Dairy Queen called mellorine. There would be sad laughter, and the telling of hard-luck stories would begin, each teller unfurling a tale of hardship that somehow outdid the last through exuberance. They brought up feelings of nostalgia and disenchantment in an uncomfortable, sometimes tense blend—missing the bad old days. Or sometimes they were complementary to the last story told—delicately coming up alongside it without overshadowing it, a way, maybe, to show deference to the last teller.

Miss Linda remembered picking cotton across the South during her childhood in the 1940s. Her family were itinerant workers who couldn't afford so much as a loaf of bread. They relied on their wits, sometimes having to steal, and the kindness of strangers. One Christmas, in a small town somewhere in the Deep South, some kind people from a local church brought them a holiday meal. She remembers her mother crying in the kitchen of the family's rented shack, grateful but devastated to have to accept charity. They had been living on poke salad, a dish made from poke-weed leaves gathered from the yard that had to be thrice boiled to remove the toxins.

Miss Linda's story prompted many of the others to share their own hard-luck stories. What seemed to hold all of them together was a sense of bewilderment at trying to talk about the contemporary in the same way. The badness of those days was at least recognizable to them; now, badness was in the air and you couldn't get a grip on it. There didn't seem to be any way out of it. It wasn't a time "in-filled with the desire of remembered loss," like the hard-luck stories of their youth spent in backbreaking labor, or anything that had a lesson to be learned at the end; no breaks for lemonade in the shade of a live oak made by the boss's kind wife.[5] It was too immediate, not thinkable as something to be yearned for later. There were no bootstraps to pull oneself up by anymore. The young people were lazy, they were on meth, they were having too many babies, and foreigners were taking their jobs away. But, at the same time, there weren't any jobs. Their children were like zombies, attached to devices, but at the same time they were too needy, too present, there were too many of them. The world was crashing down around them and they didn't care, but at the same time they complained too much. Miss Tina's own son had marriage and addiction troubles; he left his wife and moved somewhere way out in the Big Thicket with his two young daughters. Miss Tina tried to move in to help him with cooking the meals and getting the girls ready for school and church, but he would come in drunk and angry at all hours of the night, and once he pushed her down in the bathroom when she told him he wasn't doing right by those kids. He had been such a happy boy. Something had just gone sour in America. Politics and religion and the economy and daily life were all gnarled up in a knot, like a cypress knee you'd find out in the SE Texan swamps—wrapped around itself and stuck in the mud.

American fantasies of the good life still managed to play out beneath the banners of smoke in this niche social ecology.[6] The plague and profit of industry always loomed, but on mornings around Miss Tina's trailer, they got wrapped into the chuckling and the sad shaking of heads. The blast of oppressive heat was dealt with in some miracle of calm, the patient dabbing a bandana on their neck. The metaphor of America now, carrying on despite impending death—even more than this, *because of* or *with* death's threat—was too evident to pass over. It was the structure of the ecology, inhabitants locked in a stuck relationship to their world. Too tired to leave, but also nowhere to go. Made sick and exhausted and angry from the air and water and bad feelings and poverty, and fashioning a repertoire of expressivity and hard-luck stories from this suffering, yet fiercely loyal should any criticism be leveled against the place.

Strange Time

Temporality is a significant device in hard-luck stories. The passing of time becomes deliberately obscured in them, which results in the actual moment of stories being unclear. The use of the word *whenever*, for instance, as I quickly learned, was an element of Deep South temporal scenes. A young man visiting relatives, not a usual member of the RV park's morning coffee circle, used it to preface a riposte to one of Ronnie the maintenance man's long yarns, whose theme was always the sensible nature of paranoia. Ronnie said: "Can't ever be too careful when these hurricanes roll in every couple of years. Why nothin' gets built up. Wouldn't be worth it, and there ain't no time to do it. Another hurricane just gonna roll through, fuck it all up." That pregnant silence—some of the ladies viewed these rants as a bit embarrassing and smiled coolly into the glare of the grass until he got back onto the tractor mower and went on. Then they would *bless his heart* and make concessions to southern Louisiana—the exuberance of Morgan City folks—where his people came from. But then the young man, who had walked up and sheepishly stood about while the old-timers yarned, started in: "Whenever I was eight, we had a church group that built the church back up real good and some houses after the hurricane. My dad refused to evacuate, and we lived on a generator for two weeks." He was making a point that there are people who build things back up after calamities— whenever he was eight, he bore witness to this.[7] Miss Tina and the rest then enthusiastically began on this thread. The ladies located a "when" in the young man's "whenever" and rolled with it. He was talking about Hurricane Rita in 2005, which hit just after Katrina. On more than one occasion, SE Texans expressed resentment at having to live in the shadow of Katrina; they felt that the media made light of *their* hurricane.

Trump's name didn't appear until after the primary, in either the signage or the morning coffee chat. But once he got there, he stuck. He became a rehearsed preamble; once his name was invoked, the tongue was freed to release bile, long bottled up in the pent-up guts of decent white American folks (as William S. Burroughs would have it) who had had it up to here with being walked on. The position of the scarred warrior became tethered to political futurity—a way out. They wanted a sea change. Sometimes it was even expressed through the metaphor of flood or draining—a great wave to wash away the badness and the stuckness and "drain the swamp" and clean this place up and give us our jobs back and restore faith. Cruz didn't bolster them in the same way, somehow. They needed to watch someone act it out, not a politician. A brazen voice, silencing reporters, controlling mobs with ease, kicking "libtards" out of rallies, shattering all the sacred PC cows by defiling the soiled nest of diversity that liberalism created. They wanted to "Make America Great Again." Suddenly that mantra was available to them; it was a repository for all of their unfettered anger and resentment—a moral endpoint—all of this was *for* something. A great flood, like in the Bible. They didn't know they'd soon be getting Hurricane Harvey.

Harvey devastated SE Texas, as did Rita and Ike before him. In Rita, people died in their cars trying to get out, and dogs were set loose who still roamed around the Piney Woods in feral packs. Rita washed houses away with people clinging onto roofs and yelling out phone numbers to call, swept away before anyone could do anything to help. But "whenever" lent the whole thing a bit of mystery. "Whenever I was eight" referred to a fixed temporal period that had gone strange in the remembering, as though there wasn't a moment in which the young man could recall his being eight— whenever that was. He knew he was at some point eight, but he couldn't fix that time in place. It was a time indescribable as a point—the whole year of his "eightness" came into play. Whenever I was eight, the whole time. Somewhere back there.

Somebody else picked up on it: "Whenever we were kids, they used to put on great big parties, and people would dance to records. Not like now when they're all on their phones." They were on a roll with it. Miss Linda, whom everyone went silent for when she spoke, due to the quiet and the stillness in her voice (the schooled cadence of it suffused with a subtle smoker's rasp) and due to her advanced age, made the case for tornados being the real danger as far as natural disasters are concerned:

> Whenever that big one hit my brother's house up in Arkansas, well it took the whole neighborhood out. My brother and his wife hid out in the stone fireplace, only thing left standing—and all the while they're callin' and callin' for my nephew Brandon who's dumb—people say mute nowadays. Brandon don't speak at all, y'see. Well, he says "yes" sometimes, but nothin' else. Now whenever that tornado quit, they finally crawled out of the fireplace, and they were sure he was gone. Started pickin' through the piles of bricks that used to be their house, found some flashlights. Well, and after a few minutes, wouldn't you know it, here come Brandon. Just walked up out of the blue, holdin' a volleyball. And they won't never know what happened to him because he don't speak!

After a summer of this talk, I could never go back to hearing "when I was" without wincing. The fixity, the cocky assuredness of that temporal setting is too jarring, too sure of itself. In or around the time in question is the preferred mode of easing a listener into the narrative, giving them something like a cloud to rest in, instead of a line to follow, and sends them drifting. It is a synthesis with the regional folkloric form, the Texas tall tale, which always dwells in a frame of strange time. Besides, the perpetuity of "whenever" is a much more accurate descriptor for the "hanging around" quality of the impasse itself, as well as the cyclical quality of economic and natural disasters, which seem to hit the region on a "whenever" schedule. Hurricanes hit every few years and lock the region in a never-ending relationship with disaster. As Ronnie the maintenance man noted, this has had a direct effect on the quality of life. The hurricanes have prevented anything from being built up or repaired properly, thus keeping the region locked in an infrastructural plateau. This was the way people talked about Port Arthur. I noticed a marked difference in the quality of municipal and commercial buildings along the highways. They were low and nearly windowless—a uniform sandstone of squat boxes. It was as if they were squatting in preparation for the storm. After a hurricane hits and the floodwaters recede, you can drive up the highway and see the flood-line marking along the trunks of the trees—a surreal brown stain on the lower half of the trunks that goes on for miles. After Harvey, people waded around in the floodwaters for days. Many of the refineries were offline in the ensuing power loss, causing locals to speculate that there had been clandestine, deliberate leaks of toxic chemicals into the air and water.

Brian Blanchfield considers the sensation of time getting strange, which I understand, as expressed through hard-luck stories, as a state of dwelling within the perpetuity of the confounding event: "In confoundedness, the bottom has been obscured or has fallen out altogether. Clarification may yet be an antidote to confusion, the confused person understands, but the promise of bewilderment's finitude, the basic assurance that 'this too shall pass,' has dropped from confoundedness. So it is a form of suffering."[8]

The primary sensibility of the hard-luck story is a shared reeling, a feeling in which the orientations of those who have witnessed its telling have been left askew. This is how stories from a residual culture become emergent. They perform an act of presenting the world that they are in and making it vibrant. They leave us in the now of how things are. They also sometimes point to the toughness and strength of the character who has gotten through it, but not always. The random appearance of something like "redemption" made me hesitate. I couldn't just loop the hard-luck stories into an explanation of them as a microcosm: "The Story of America" wasn't continuing smoothly, and it wasn't ending happily. The stories were bigger than that.

One older man, a morning coffee semi-regular, ritualistically finished his time in the story circle by slowly rising, gathering his crossword, and waving his hand dismissively at the confabulations, relieving himself of the accrual of bad feeling. One morning, feeling salty, he turned back and said something about the end coming: "None of us'll be around to see it, anyway." Then he walked up the two steps into his trailer and shut the door against the heat and the bad air and the rest of them, sitting around telling stories about the perpetual badness of their world.

The Landlord

In a rare moment of seriousness, the landlord asked me: "What could you do to make this place better? Probably bulldoze the whole damn thing, start over." We were driving down North Main Street in Vidor, six miles east of Beaumont. It was the template of the depressed American town, a familiar scene that has etched itself into the American consciousness: strip malls dotted with gas stations and fast-food joints unbroken for about a two-and-a-half mile stretch, interrupted only by the strange town hall, which was a new, well-groomed facility—one of the only ones. The city hall functioned primarily as a shrine to Vidorians, such as the late George Jones, who once shot the landlord's cousin in the butt as he was fleeing from a window after being caught in bed with Jones's wife.[9] The two men later became good friends.

Besides the city hall, everything else was covered in the film of disuse and a looming rage that is peculiar to the history of this place. On that day, a large group of bikers gathered in the parking lot at Whataburger— pronounced the Texas way: *Water-Burger*. The landlord was speaking about his fellow Vidorians; he had moved away from Vidor but still owned properties there. There was the general impression that things were destroyed: "They tore up that playground in McDonald's, ripped the whole damn thing out." We pulled up to the drive-thru line at Dairy Queen to get some Blizzards. "You know they have to turn 'em upside down when they give 'em to you, and if anything comes out, it's free!" He seemed to get a lot of pleasure from this. As we waited, he reflected on old Vidor, his mode of storytelling building a memory house, a catalog of characters in which ghosts screaming with laughter dwelt. A SE Texas lost to him, lost to everyone. Suspended in time, circling the track in a late-1950s roller rink, Santo and Johnny's "Sleepwalk" blasting over the loud system:

Man, when I was a kid, this place was different. There was stuff to do! My Aunt Pearl had a roller rink, and we'd spend near every day there after school let out. Put peanuts in our Dr. Pepper back then. World was different. Aunt Pearl sat up in the office and smoked, looking down on everything. She let us get away with so much. Man, we just about went wild! And I was the best skater in town—man, can you picture me? What a cool kid! Doing tricks, skating backwards, music blasting, that disco ball. It was special. And the people! There was Skeeter, Collarbutton, Bobby Jones—Skeeter was this lil' ol' guy—skinny and such a character. He was a great skater— older fella, you know. Was just always around. But he'd be popping and twirling and pulling faces at the girls, doing crazy eyebrow stuff. Smilin' like a possum eatin' persimmon. We had a great time out there. And now look at this place. Man, it's rough. All there is to do is fight. And these Vidor women are rough. They love to fight.

He left the story in a reeling place, a place of closed-down pockets of happiness and exuberance. He chuckled sadly, shook his head, and sipped his Blizzard. The ice cream drink was not yet soft enough to make it up the straw, so his face became red and sunken with the labor of sucking.

Petro-Texas

This is the Refinery Belt, the heart of the US petrochemical industry, a locus of America's petroculture culture of poetics, nostalgia, and longing. Stephanie Lemanager calls the feelings associated with this culture "petronostalgia," both a lamenting and a longing for the phantom promises and lost "good old days" of extractive industry's prosperity.[10] Here, strange, eccentric, and tough characters populate the stories of Texan industry that propelled the state out of rurality: the merciless, self-made Pattillo Higgins; the conman oil wildcatter Columbus Marion "Dad" Joiner, the rumor-plagued industrialist H. J. Lutcher Stark, the matronly dowager shut-in Mamie McFaddin Ward. Above all, these rebel speculators and weird aristocrats are bound up in the mythic pursuit and conquest of that black gold, oil, that has dictated the mercurial life of boom-or-bust Texas from the beginning of its history and has led to it being overtaken by the shady and dangerous dealings of the fracking industry, which blankets nearly the whole state.

The Texas Oil Boom officially began on January 10, 1901, in Beaumont, with the notorious "Prophet of Spindletop" Pattillo Higgins, a crooked businessman who, in 1880, at the age of seventeen, lost his arm in a gunfight with a sheriff's deputy after harassing a local Black Baptist church. The deputy died from his wounds, but Higgins was acquitted on grounds of self-defense and sent off to work as a one-armed logger on the Texas–Louisiana border. He found Jesus in 1885 and came back home to Beaumont. He taught himself geology and speculated that there was oil in the Sour Hill Mound, a stinking sulfurous salt dome mound just south of town.[11] Undeterred by mockery from the local papers, Higgins partnered with mining engineer Captain Anthony Lucas and began drilling, striking oil on January 10 at about 1,020 feet. Higgins had speculated that the oil was one thousand feet below ground; according to legend, he pulled this number out of thin air and was badly mocked for it. His team's trailblazing practices, such mudding the sides of the well to form a protective sediment and using new drilling devices such as rotary bits, created the template for contemporary oil drilling.

Spindletop's Lucas gusher was an unprecedented burst of oil from the earth, producing three million barrels of oil in its first year, and over seventeen million barrels the second year. After barely a week, the stranglehold monopoly on oil held by the Yankee John D. Rockefeller's Standard Oil was upended. Higgins ended up suing Captain Lucas and the Gladys Oil Company, which they had formed together for royalties, using lease technicalities to win his case. He then formed his own oil company and spent the rest of his days establishing other wells with different investors. Higgins was a teetotaler who was against swimming and dancing, believing that man could "achieve moral perfection on Earth."[12] He didn't marry until he was forty-five, to an eighteen-year-old girl named Annie Jahn, whom he had adopted in 1905 when she was fifteen. They had three children. He died in 1955 in San Antonio at the age of ninety-one.

The birth of cheap Texas oil marked the acceleration of an epoch. Framed in contemporary terms, it was the major event of the beginning of the second Industrial Revolution. The mythic quality of this moment cannot be overstated: the moment when our dependence on fossil fuels sprang into high gear, sending us headlong into the impasse of now. This history positions the region as the perfect culprit for the murder of our planet, and journalists, climate change scholars, theorists, and environmentalists use the Texas oil boom as an origin point in a genealogy of disaster, marked by the major events of the twenty-first century: the modern ecological crisis, the sixth extinction event, the intractable acceleration of the Anthropocene.

At the time of my fieldwork, SE Texas was inhabited by multiple vast oil refinery complexes. The six largest refineries in the United States are located along the Refinery Belt from Texas to Louisiana. The ExxonMobil Baytown Refinery, the second largest refinery in the United States, produces on average 560,500 barrels of petroleum a day. Out in the Golden Triangle sits the largest refinery in North America, and the fifth-largest in the world: the Saudi Aramco Port Arthur Refinery, which can produce more than 600,000 barrels a day. The refineries bear the legacies of the oil barons and wildcatters like Higgins, whose efforts led to the creation of the great companies, Gulf Oil and Texaco, and who still today haunt the tangles of tubing, the spouts of fire and smoke, the refineries that have the power to change the sky green, as Mary Karr famously noted in *The Liars' Club*.[13] The Port Arthur Refinery was Texaco's first refinery, opened in 1903. Standard Oil opened Beaumont's ExxonMobil Refinery in 1902. These complexes, looming behind their fences, compound the heat, turn it into something more than felt: it is breathed, it is lived. This atmosphere kills while the bodies of sE Texans labor inside of the refineries' bowels, on their rigging and stairwells, standing over their great vats and basins and occasionally falling into them, burned by flash fires, crushed by falling containers, killed in explosions—forced to accept the constant danger and baseline of precarious health these labor conditions cause.[14]

The Trailer Park

The landlord grew up in Vidor. He was on the football team and very popular in town. When he married, he moved his family to a small trailer park that he had inherited from his parents by the railroad tracks, where, over the years, he expanded a trailer into a larger house by adding slapdash renovations and additions until the structure was no longer recognizable as a trailer. At the time of my fieldwork, he would come down from his house in the country in Jasper County every week to mow the lawns, make small repairs, collect rent money, and hang out with the tenants to make small talk. He had a camaraderie with his tenants that is rare. He advised them on life decisions, drank Bud Light with them sometimes, and generally kept the peace. He was a character in the realest sense of the word—full of exuberance, with stories both dreadful and hilarious about his time in the trailer park, his job at the natural gas plant in Orangefield, and the town of Vidor and its history. He only took me to the trailer park a few times, once telling me that I couldn't hang out there for more than a few minutes because the tenants would "eat you alive." So, most of my knowledge of the trailer park tenants came from his stories. It was at first a frustrating limitation, but I soon realized that the quality of these character studies was a craftsmanship of mythic proportions—in the landlord's telling, the tenants were mythic characters, larger than life, bursting out of their archetypal modes in moments of crazed exuberance and dysfunction. The truth of the stories mattered less than the effect of their reeling intensities.

Vidor was a repository for these intensities. It had maintained a forbidden aura that went beyond its reputation from the days of the Klan. Its isolation produced an excess of stories that were comfortable sitting untethered from the duress of having to be sensible or moderate. It was as though a corner of the garden, neglected by the gardener, had grown masses and entanglements. Character cultivated in this unchecked corner proliferated unexpectedly. People burst or sag out of their ordinary lives in portraits of rage and abjection: stabbings in parking lots came as no surprise, and a pig that nobody seemed to own kept showing up at the 7-Eleven. They called him Bacon and fed him Wonder Bread. Neighbors and neighborliness might take a strange turn; there were whisperings of neighbors having died and left the house to their children who were on meth or God knows what. They hollowed out the house and spent all hours of the night carrying on. Used to be, a neighbor was neighborly.

Walmart ("Wally World" to the landlord) was expanding into a Supercenter; its parking lot spread across the town. People were allowed to camp out there in RVs. There were hookups in some places, and people felt safe under the floodlights. They did all their shopping at Walmart, and now had attached themselves to it more permanently.

Walmart bought out everyone except for one old lady who refused to budge. She was holding out in her little house, her rightful property. They built the parking lot around her house, surrounding her on all sides. They hadn't even left her a patch of grass to stand on. People said she was admirable and brave to stand her ground like that; others called her stupid, old, and stubborn. She'd be gone soon enough, anyway, then they'd knock down the house. Or whoever inherited her house might take up the cause—if there was anyone. Stubbornness is one of those traits that reappear in stories about people who stick to something and won't quit.

The Oscar-winning 2017 film *Three Billboards outside Ebbing, Missouri* is allegedly based on billboards that stood on I-10 as it passed through Vidor. The elderly father of a murder victim, Kathy Page, a white woman whose murder remains unsolved, maintained the signs. Page was found dead in her car with no obvious wounds or damage to the vehicle, what police speculated was a staged car wreck. According to Page's father, and to most anyone I spoke to in town, she was murdered by her husband, Steve Page, in 1991. Steve spoke to the police, maintaining his innocence but conveying a bizarre affect. He would be crying and throw himself down on the couch sobbing, but then would immediately stand up and begin speaking to them again without any tears in his eyes. Later, when attention on him intensified, he told the Vidor police that a member of the Beaumont mafia had murdered his wife. A whole network of stories related to the Kathy Page murder still circulated in Vidor. A woman at the RV park told me that a swatch of the carpet in the Pages' home had been cut out and disposed of by Steve; he told police that Kathy had been frying fish on the floor and ruined the carpet with grease. The billboards blamed the Vidor police for executing a cover-up, suggesting a conspiracy of flubbed investigations and turning the other way. The most famous and consistently present one read: "Steve Page brutally murdered his wife in 1991—Vidor P.D. does not want to solve this case—I believe they took a bribe—The Attorney general should investigate—James Fulton—her father." The signs changed over the years, but at a certain point, one of the billboards included a photograph of Steve Page desecrating Kathy's grave, kicking flowers from it in a rage. I often wonder if the misremembering of the racist billboard had something to do with these signs, which did something much more than tell you about the Page incident. They enveloped you back into the idea of death every time you passed through. It seems possible that other, more diabolical signs could have been dreamt up in the process of collective memory that a community engages in together. Then again, it seems just as likely that a billboard telling Black people to stay out would have fit in perfectly with the excessive, negatively exuberant atmospheres on the Vidor patch of the great interstate.

The landlord's stories about his tenants at the trailer park were almost always funny; they always contained elements of humor and ended with laughter. However, it was the quality of his laughter, which must be described as dark, that complicated my suspicion that he was mocking the subjects of his stories. A disconnected quality was at work, in which tragic content was treated with a humorous form. I refer to this storytelling mode as comic abjection, drawing from ideas about disorder that define qualities of the abject subject, the trailer park character, as speaking from a place of badness and embodying what is pitiable to the most extreme degree.[15] The humorous framing is not meant as a way of downplaying the tragic, but of tending to the accrual of the tragic and engaging with what Brian Reed, in his S-Town podcast, calls the "fuck it" mentality of the poor whites he encountered in smalltown Alabama. Barbara Ching considers what comes after the "fuck it," the resultant culture as an expressivity that exceeds nihilism, and explores the exuberant quality that crafts a poetic language out of badness. Ching calls it "burlesque abjection" in the hard country genre, noting that "if you are down so low that your only hope is a new ideal, applauding the burlesque can give subversive pleasure."[16]

Julia Kristeva notes that there are materials closely associated with the abject, one of them being excrement—a substance that "stand[s] for the danger to identify that comes from without: the ego threatened by the non-ego, society threatened by its outside, *life by death*."[17] While several of the stories do in fact involve excrement, such as a story about a severed septic line that created a "shit geyser," the association of abjection with excrement is more metaphorically constructed within the shittiness of life almost universally shared in the repertoire of SE Texan stories. Similar to the *S* in *S-Town* standing for shit, these stories do more than abhor what Mary Douglas famously called "disordered systems."[18] They acknowledge the shitty as an integral quality to the building up of character: dark laughter at the ever-looming threat of death, disorder, and badness. The stories harness these elements, building a character fluent in the grotesque as an expressive form. In this incommensurability, the disparate nature between the stuck and the vibrantly grotesque is a relationship to nihilism that is more complicated than the narrative of a destructive life, hell-bent on self-eradication. The "fuck it" mentality is not necessarily constituted by apathy; the comic abjection of the trailer park hard-luck stories are doing much more than just giving up.

In Mikhail Bakhtin's taxonomy of grotesquerie, "the grotesque body is a body of becoming. It is never finished, never completed."[19] The grotesqueness of comic abjection means that the abject character is stuck in this relation of becoming, fostered by the conditions of what is being grappled with—in this case, with the daily conditions of the trailer park. The landlord allowed his tenants some freedom, within reason. They could be late with the rent, gather at the end of the street to deal and buy drugs, and drink and become rowdy. Each person was an abject character, and in combination there was great chaos, which the landlord reveled in until it became an issue.

The trailer park had no name. It was called "the trailer park," or just "the park," by the landlord. The house across the street from the park had a name. It was called the Glidewell (*glahd-will*) house, in strangely reverent tones, because that was the last name of the old couple who lived there for years. After Mrs. Glidewell passed, Mr. Glidewell was just too tired to go on and "died of a broken heart" a few months later. The landlord sometimes called the trailer park by the name of the street it was on—a dirt road off of the Old Spanish Trail.

The cicadas were deafening in high summer. The quality of the air is difficult to describe, but, as with most of the region, it hung heavy with the ill effects of the refineries and caused the dusk glow in the summer. The air itself could sometimes burn. The landlord liked to say that if you drove your car into the trailer park, a group of the tenants would be sitting around a decrepit picnic set, surrounded by piles of beer cans and liquor bottles, cigarette butts, broken cars, toys, washing machines, and so on, on the bare patch of earth under the relentless Texas sun that was their common space.

Some others would come out of their trailers to see who had arrived; they might be welcoming or threatening. The majority of the tenants were on social welfare programs, and the landlord seemed to imply that "waiting on their SSI checks" was one of the only markers of temporality, of entering back into time at the park. In the landlord's stories, the tenants were always gathered, sitting idly in strange time, and yet their world did not suggest pastoral idleness, a way of slowing down or enjoying life. When the landlord asked his tenants how their day was going or what they were doing, there were a range of answers, some humorous, that suggested a violent and pregnant rurality, a looming and nihilistic pastoral. The landlord later told me that there was a tenant named James Brown. He was the cleanest tenant, and the landlord laughed about his name, repeating it for effect: "Yep, that's his name: James Brown. *James Brown.*"

There was an older woman whom the landlord never named, but he told me about the track marks on her legs where she had been shooting up Dilaudid, a popular and powerful opioid used for patients who have developed a tolerance for other opioids. The landlord described the woman as a heavy smoker whose laughter erupted into coughing fits that took minutes to recover from.

One woman was the topic of most of the stories. Her nickname was Fuzzy. She had lived in the trailer park for many years but was, fantastically, originally from Brooklyn, New York. My assumption, though this was never broached, was that the other tenants called her Fuzzy for racist reasons; she appeared to be mixed race, and the name was a reference to her hair. Yet she wore the nickname with a reluctant pride. Her trailer was filled with cockroaches—I was told that they covered every surface. She was "et up with 'em," the popular phrase to describe this situation. Her sons were wayward; she lamented them as though they were dead and had pictures of them. The landlord told me that Fuzzy's family was "coonass," which was what people in SE Texas and Louisiana regularly called people of Cajun ethnicity. It was also an emic term. Multiple folk etymologies make it mysterious and difficult to verify. Most people I asked about the origin maintained that it had nothing to do with the racial slur "coon." In defense of this position, the landlord referred to a bumper sticker that I had seen: "Registered Coonass: ain't worryin' bout nothin'," with a raccoon in sunglasses reclining on a pool float. He told me, "Well, y'see, back a long time ago, the Cajuns around here were pelters. They hung those raccoons up on their front porches by their tails, by their asses. That's where it comes from."

The landlord referred to visiting his trailer park as "messin' with my people." It was a variation on "visitin' with," and always seemed to me to suggest a more active companionship. Something almost collaborative. He savored the falling out of time with them, sat with them for hours, laughing and telling strange and fantastic stories about another time. I noticed that his accent became more Vidorian when he was speaking with them on the phone or even about them; his mannerisms became more severe. He assembled the trailer park characters in his stories as you might discuss museum pieces—curious objects, exquisitely formed, open to speculative interpretations. Their temporality was the strange time of the ever-present. They could be evoked as if he had just seen them the other day, but in fact, might not have heard of them in decades. He left them in weird, confounded places, ending his stories with a shrug or a half-speculated explanation of what might have happened to them, what bad fate they might have met. It was as though they could be waiting just around the next corner. The scene he set was always one of terrible severity, the town of Vidor being a place beyond help. He often said that the only way to fix Vidor would be to "bulldoze everything down, start over." He evoked the inhabitants of Vidor, himself included on occasion, as uncivilized to the point of being feral: the words he used were rough, the way one might describe animals. He described Vidor women as "loving to fight," and Vidor itself as sitting outside the purview of the social.

The landlord's favorite story, which he told repeatedly as though for the first time, was about a former tenant he referred to as "Heard Dat." The man was an exceptional tenant apart from the fact that the only words he seemed to utter were "heard dat" in response to whatever had just been said, although the literalness of the utterance was hard to grasp. It was impossible to know whether the man was expressing agreement with some deeper sentiment or merely asserting that he had heard whatever had been said. He was handy with tools and would help out with repairs and chores, but he mostly just stood around. Evidently, Heard Dat eventually took to "drinkin' and druggin' and hangin' around with bad news people" and disappeared from the trailer park for some months. After the landlord had not heard from him for an amount of time he deemed the limit, he cleared Heard Dat's belongings out of his trailer, and cleaned and prepared it for the next tenant: "Well, one mornin' after a couple of months, here comes Heard Dat in his truck. He just rolled up like nothing happened and he hadn't been gone, y'know. I walked out there on the porch and just told him 'Hell no, man, turn around. You don't have a place here no more.' He just goes 'Heard dat!' [He] turned his truck around and drove out. That's all the motherfucker ever said! [*laughs*] I never seen him again after that."

Bicycle John was the central culprit of the chaos in the trailer park. He was always drunk, and would ride wobbling into the park on his rusty bike with some great scheme for making fast money. Or he'd be winding people up, going around looking in their windows and dancing, getting very close to them when he spoke, or spreading rumors. He didn't live in the trailer park. Bicycle John's girlfriend was Fuzzy, whose trailer the landlord eventually "condemned" for being too filthy and filled with cockroaches. She didn't seem to mind; she laughed it off when the eviction was taken up by the many wild storytellers in the little park community. She mostly sat calmly in her lawn chair, watching what happened. She was kind and childlike. The one time I spoke to her was at a funeral. She had made a pretty little cross from straw and gave it to the mourners, whose mother had died. The landlord saw her as a good watcher and knew he could rely on her and Bicycle John to tell him what was going on in the park. "They may be nasty, but they're not thieves," the landlord said about the unruly couple, as well as about a lot of his tenants. On many days, Bicycle John would get out-of-control drunk, and Fuzzy had to put him to bed in her trailer to avoid trouble. The landlord went on exceedingly expressive rants about Bicycle John in a tone of admiration mixed with revulsion, repeating his nickname:

> Man, he rides his bicycle all around that damn trailer park! He's real, real hairy and drunk all the time. I run him off every now and then, but he always comes back. Ol' Bicycle John. [*laughs*] Looks like a damn werewolf. I was cuttin' grass one day and yelled at him and waved, and he didn't know who the hell it was. Too damn drunk. He reached back and tried to dig his can of Skoal out, and he ended up rollin' all on the ground tryin' to get it out. [*laughs*] Then ol' Fuzzy come out of trailer number five and started yellin' at him with that big hair and little chihuahua. She's a mess. Ain't hurtin' anything though . . . One day ol' John rode that bicycle straight in the creek back there. Guess he missed the turn or something. Cops don't even bring him to jail anymore, they just load him up and take him back to his mama. I gotta run him off when I got people comin' to look at a trailer. Ain't nobody gonna rent one when they step out and see a damn werewolf.

The trailer park was constituted by a web of abject relations that suspended it in the perpetual hard-luck scene. Tenants made just enough to eke out a life there, but they were too poor to move on. Most of them collected welfare and social security checks, which structured their month-to-month precarity. Addiction and mental health issues went unchecked and untreated. On the first of the month, they would pool their SSI and welfare checks and head out to Houston to the "pill mills," as the landlord called them: pain management centers in the great Houston exurban sprawl where they can more easily score prescriptions for Xanax, Oxycontin, and Dilaudid. There was an element of manipulation in play during these schemes. The landlord told of times when the senior citizens' checks were taken from them under duress or outright stolen from them, after which the younger trailer park residents scored prescriptions to abuse or to sell at the end of the road. The seniors never saw any of the profits from these schemes, but they didn't go to the police due to a general sense of distrust and a fear of punishment. One senior, referred to as "the old man" by the residents, had a few of his checks taken this way. There were suspicions that some of the other residents were opening his mail. He slept in a chair in his trailer most days and could be seen catching the sun through the window. One day, the landlord stood for a few minutes watching him, convinced he was dead: "But he was only sleeping, he just had his mouth *way open*, you know."

Dangerous events occurred at least partially as a result of the illicit scheming and drug activity in the trailer park. One young man, high on meth, drove out onto the railroad tracks that ran parallel to the park's perimeter. He was hit in his car. The train pushed him for half a mile before it was able to stop. He survived but was never the same. His speech and affect were more slurred. He sold weed at the end of the road and drifted in and out of the park, staying with different people around town. People said that he had gotten what was coming to him, yet much of their own behavior matched his nearly to a tee.

The feeling was that they were all living in a moral in-between state, in which their activities were not judged on a local, immediate, or interpersonal level. But they were always under the scrutiny of some immaterial tribunal. This was a common frame among the folks I hung around with in SE Texas. The tribunal was not always God, but would be worded as God or a "higher power" if people were pressed to identify what was watching them. "There's just a way that life gets back at you," one man told me. Being an abject character meant entering into this stuck relationship with the world—being autonomous to the extent that you make choices for yourself, but being aware of the intractable pathways that people get on, grooves that lives get locked into in fulfillment of narratives and stories that are already there, succumbing to the catalog of possibilities that characters recognize and participate in as stories. Becoming a character can mean getting stuck in a place, having an unsettled belonging to a place where you don't' quite fit. You make sense there, but only in a frustrating way in which you are constantly feeling the frayed edges of your daily existence.

Characters have their place. If pushed to justify his tolerance of Bicycle John, the landlord would tell a story about another bicycle-riding eccentric called Collarbutton who was a local character during the landlord's childhood in the 1960s in Vidor. Collarbutton was so called because "he buttoned his shirt all the way up to the collar." He could be seen daily riding his bike the six miles or so from Vidor into Beaumont, where he held some mysterious job repairing objects. He was also an ace bike repairman, and the neighborhood kids would bring their bicycles to him, which he could always fix without question and in a matter of minutes. There was some exuberant element to him, mental illness of some sort, the poor going largely undiagnosed in those days and in that place. The landlord would do an impression of him, arms high up on handlebars, eyes crossed, weaving haplessly to and fro on his bike as though the bike might stray off into a ravine—a person who stumbles onto the scene. "Saw him get hit by a car once. Whoa, Collarbutton! You alright, man? He just got up and took off like nothin' happened. Who knows where he is now . . . Probably dead."

Fuzzy and Bicycle John were characters who were stuck in the space of the trailer park. Although class and education play a large part in this stuckness, these factors merely explain a condition. They do not grasp the profundity of stuckness as a way of life that exceeds the causal, that describes the atmosphere of that experience as more than just something unfortunate. One morning, the landlord told me a story about the only Black tenant who ever lived in the trailer park: "She was real tough, arms out to here, and I really admired her for stickin' it out down there with those rough people." Evidently, the woman worked at a factory nearby and was dating a white woman in Vidor. The tenants expressed discontent, but the landlord told them to mind their manners. "Well, one day she laid Bicycle John out. He must have come up and talked some shit, y'know, got in her face. Said some racist stuff. Well, she just knocked his ass flat. Nobody messed with her after that. Tough. And she was real clean and paid her bills on time. She didn't stay much longer after that though." Her story is a reminder of the incommensurable event that binds people to place and to each other in uncomfortable ways: racism explains the context, but the feeling of this encounter becomes too much, in excess of any logical explanation. People become characters, and while this title is usually reserved for others ("she was a real character"), it can also grasp and hold the self in its thrall.

Having coffee with the landlord and his wife, Deb, one morning, the usual recap of all of the trailer park characters was interrupted. Deb said: "Are you gonna tell him about the pedophile?" The landlord grinned in his mischievous way and told me that a pedophile had come to live in the trailer park recently. He said that the police had circulated notices that a sex offender was moving into the park, but Deb corrected him. The young man himself was required by law to circulate cards in the trailer park that identified him as a sex offender. It wasn't long before tenants began lodging complaints with the landlord, who expressed concern for the young man's safety. "After all, it was just something he did when he was a kid, when he was twelve. Touched a younger cousin or something like that. It isn't like he goes around raping kids or anything. And he's clean, and he pays his rent—we've got him living with the old guy down there who fixes up the trailers, and he's a good handyman. Better than my last one."

When I told the landlord that his life seemed to be populated by characters of all sorts, he went silent for a moment. "People *are* characters," he told me, and then launched into a story he'd been meaning to tell me about a man called Quentin Dew whom I had heard him mention previously. I have transcribed the short story in full, as it seems to get at the textural quality of character in the way the landlord understood that term to function:

> I was workin' with this big, big fat guy, and all he done was tell jokes and stuff, and he'd talk about how they were underpaid and all that kinda shit, and—*he was comical.* He might do a job, and he might talk nearly all day and put up two sheets of panelin', you know. His name was Quentin Dew. They sent me over there to work with him—they warned me about him— he, he said, "How long you been with the company?" And I said, "I just started." And he said, "You'll learn." [*laughs*] I said, "Okay"—and so, he was puttin' flooring down, in the house. And, uh, I got to goin' a little bit too fast for him, ya know? And he said, "Hold it!" He said, "You know, I'ma make a pretty damn good helper here after a while." [*laughs*] And that meant that I was goin' too fast. But, uh, that guy told joke after joke after joke. One day he come to work out there, and see, he worked all over because they had company housing—back then they had carpenters. They had like one carpenter per district—cos they had the housing and stuff that

they kept up—he come to work out there—well, his cousin Homer was an old operator out there, and he come to put storm doors on the houses. He said, "I tell you." He said, "I've got all right-handed doors," and he said, "That's really what you're goin' there." But he said, "I'll be damned when I get down there to Homer and Lavinia's, they gonna want a left-handed door." He said, "You watch and see what I'm tellin' you." And they did want a left-hand door. [*laughs*] And he got all mad, said . . . He come back the next mornin' and he was all flustered and stuff, and, uh, he dropped a pencil or something, and Homer said, "Here's your pencil you dropped." And something was said, and he got mad and he said, "That makes me so goddamn mad." And he put his pencil in there and missed his pocket, and it hit the floor. He said, "I'll fix that!" and he ripped his shirt pocket off, and he said, "Now, gimme that goddamn pencil!" And he put it in there, and He said, "I tell you what." He said, "When I get like this and all shook up and people is botherin' me." He said, "I'm just gonna go to the goddamn motel and drink a beer!" And he said, "That's what I'm gon' do, bye." And he took off and went to the motel. And that was it. And our boss said, "He'll be alright tomorrow. He just gets like that." Well, see, those big shots, he was such a good carpenter and a cabinetmaker, and he was real, real good, and those big shots up there would get him to come work on their houses and stuff, see. They'd pay him under the table and shit like that. [*laughs*] Quentin Dew, D-E-W. That was his name. He's dead now.

Character Studies

What did the landlord mean when he said that everyone was a character? I took him to mean that all lives have capacious stories, that all people can become recognizable types. In the moment of telling those stories, they become characterized. To be a character is to enact the troubling mix of qualities that legitimate us to the interior, to the scene in which we dwell—but in this very gesture, what the character is to the exterior (the perceived outside) takes on a deep meaning that constitutes, in the now of the United States, a national wound. A character can be a node of badness, carrying a charge that makes people roll their eyes, turn away in revulsion or shame, or even point to the person as the source of the problem. In the affective epoch of now, what some people call, only half-jokingly, the "Trumpocene," the supposed resurgence of this character as a social presence, a thing to once again be dealt with, seems to be held up as the source of this American wound. People in SE Texas spoke of characters, either in reverent tones or as signs of warning: a person who might fly off the handle at any moment; someone stuck in a bad loop, where you know what they're going to say before they even say it because they've been saying it for years, standing outside of the 7-Eleven chain-smoking. "He's a *real* character," they might say, with a heavy suggestion in their voice that tells you to watch out. The bad feeling of character is what has stuck in the stories of our new disenfranchised "homegrown terrorists," poor rural white males like Dylann Roof, who were the subject of fascination after they committed their atrocities. Journalists went to South Carolina to unearth Roof's past: What exactly had deformed his character so severely to make him walk into a church and murder nine praying Black parishioners at a Bible study? They found a catalog of bad characters in the abject scene of the Hideaway trailer park in Columbia where he had been staying. Those people had festered alongside him in what journalists decried as nihilism, abjection, and hedonism. Roof had spent the summer on their couch. In the abject scene they wallowed in, the journalists said, his virulent racist and murderous remarks were workaday fare. They had gone unnoticed. Roof's father had given him an IOU on his birthday to buy a gun. This detail was revealed after a journalist interviewed the father, who claimed that he had no idea why his son had committed this crime; he said that his son "wasn't raised like that" and quickly ended the interview.[20] The idea was that an atmosphere had created Dylann Roof, one in which a conditioned severity was the norm, as layers of this bad life built up around him.

The coming into play of certain affective qualities heralds this moment. These qualities have messed with the way that politics happen, constituting an impasse of what can be said or done. Integral to the moment is the composition and conveyance of character, the coming together of recognizable forms drawn from media into troubled composites. The composite of the rural white, which is a mixture of the white, non-cosmopolitan (but not always non-urban), non-liberal (but not always conservative), uneducated (but not always unschooled)—finds its shorthand representation in the character.

Severity is a composition of life. It is the dwelling place of that which has somehow been drastically laid bare by suffering. In most depictions of severity, there is an accompanying humanist angle that frames and somehow justifies our fascination with it. In a series of portraits of severe faces, there might be an accompanying blurb that describes the faces as hard-working, oppressed, belonging to lives that have been "through the ringer" and that are now, in the moment of looking, being valorized or recentered from a marginalized place. The event of witnessing severity as an entrancing formal element is in this way attached to the humanist concept of suffering and so tethered back into the moral. But severity's potential exceeds something to be pitied or honored. Severity, as in the case of the storytellers and scenes of this book, can be an atmosphere that draws in those who dwell within it, setting things in stark relief and framing the world in a different way. Severity can be the mode rather than the exception.

To label something severe is not merely a value-laden statement denoting an intensity of roughness; its visual scope is broader than that. The word *severe* varies in its descriptive potential. In bodies and faces, those of humans or even nonhuman animals, severity is the utmost limit of form that a body or face can take without spilling over into something unrecognizable. The visually severe in a human face is a conglomeration of traits that push the face to the absolute end of what a face can look like. It is more of a face than you can bear. On the other side of this, a severity in an object like a house could describe the dissolution of that house's structural integrity—a "severe" house is one that is severely dilapidated or damaged. It is a house that is almost no longer a house due to the severity of whatever effects have afflicted it. It is less of a house than what is commonly called a house. It would be less common (but more artful) to hear a house described as severe in the way that a face would be described as severe. This would refer to the possibly brutalist or futurist angularity of the house's form. It would be a house whose shape pushes to the limit what a house could be. So, visually, severity is an extremity of appearance that falls on either side of an axis of recognition—it is either too much or almost not holding together.

Severity does different things. It appears to us attached to these bodies and faces, but it also spreads across the landscape and the conditions of being, called the "severity of life" in this work. The visual markers of severity are its products as a condition and a way of being. Severity as a condition marks its subjects. So, severe faces in portraiture, such as the famous Walker Evans portraits of sharecroppers that accompanied James Agee's text in *Let Us Now Praise Famous Men*, are visual catalogs of severity's accrual—the building up of hard luck into a manifestation. One of the ways that someone might explain a severe appearance is by saying, "They have *lived hard*."

Agee obsesses over this symbiotic (or is it parasitic?) relation between the literary and the "real." His work on Alabama sharecroppers is narrated by a voice that admonishes itself for its lack of space within which to *see* (and therefore to honestly depict) the tenant farmers he encounters. It is more than the creative power of fiction, Agee insists, that his endeavor demands. It is a deeply troubled dance of the real: the relation between the intimidating texture of the real people he aims to describe and the reality of his own voice's limitations. This trepidation is the kernel of the great anxiety of ethnographic writing. In his famously tempestuous, thorny, and self-flagellating introduction to the work, Agee says:

> In a novel, a house or person has his meaning, his existence, entirely through the writer. Here, a house or a person has only the most limited of his meaning through me: his true meaning is much huger. It is that he *exists*, in actual being, as you do and as I do, and as no character of the imagination can possibly exist. His great weight, mystery, and dignity are in this fact. As for me, I can tell you of him only what I saw, only so accurately as in my own terms I know how: and this in turn has its chief stature not in any ability of mine but in the fact that I too exist, not as a work of fiction, but as a human being. Because of his immeasurable weight in actual existence, and because of mine, every word I tell of him has inevitably a kind of immediacy, a kind of meaning, not at all necessarily "superior" to that of imagination, but of a kind so different that a work of the imagination (however intensely it may draw on "life") can at best only faintly imitate the least of it.[21]

Agee describes the quandary of the ethnographic, yet in so doing he strategically creates a distinction between the fictive and the real that can never be tidily kept separate. Character is not merely a property of the fictive. Character is what mutually constitutes the image of the person we create and the real qualities of the person we aim to depict—the *properties* of character are not fictional. There may be different modes of reception of these properties, and there are certainly different trajectories these properties take depending on how we spin them into motion. But because the sensible unveils phenomena, the deep distrust Agee (and the rest of us) have in our own writing and thinking processes is a paranoia having more to do with the interpretive than the perceptive.[22] What we will *do* with what we have seen is at stake, and these perceptions "becoming literary" are one of the chief elements of this paranoia. But what if the qualities that tempt us into the literary mode of thought and description about the real, as the poetic description of severity, are not distortions, but augmentations?

Character becoming recognizable has been a preoccupation of mine. It is ultimately an unanswerable question—one of those ideas that set you spinning in many directions at once. I wonder where character started, what routes recognizable forms took before being taken up by a larger culture. There is no way to tell whether character began in depiction or through which depictions. Why attribute the possible origins of character to *either* fiction or the real? There is a seduction in the desire to know that character *comes from somewhere*. The phrase "stranger than fiction" resonates here, because it implies that there are *real* phenomena that exceed the structure of what is fictive, that there are origin points in life for fictive devices that exceed them in terms of their strangeness, their specificity being too textured to be constricted within a tidy story. "You can't make this stuff up" is another apt phrase. It is saying again that what reality shows us is that, despite our best efforts to outdo it with our own creative capacities, it will always have the final say—stretching the limit of what is possible as a phenomenon to put our creations to shame. There is also the saying "larger than life," one that the landlord himself used on more than one occasion to describe his trailer park tenants, and a phrase that I would not hesitate to use in describing the landlord. It points to characters whose qualities make them exceed the boundaries of what can be understood as real; people who are larger than life have a fictive aura. The phrase reverses the idea of the real exceeding the fictive, adding another layer to the tracing of character origin, which remains an endlessly looping endeavor. The real and the fictive exceed one another in common parlance, and this cyclical relationship remains looped in productive perpetuity.

Whiteness and Hard Luck

Hard-luck stories and their characters get racialized, which is to say I found them to be yanked into the repertoire of whiteness and its attendant narratives regardless of whom the stories were about or what they suggested. Even stories about negative events that could not be accurately described as hard-luck stories, such as the stories of racially motivated killings or racist violence in SE Texas, were rerouted through this persistent narrative form. The most infuriating and marked instance of this phenomenon that I encountered in SE Texas is the horrific story of the murder of James Byrd, retold to me by countless white people in SE Texas.

In the summer of 1998, James Byrd Jr., a forty-nine-year-old Black man, was lynched by three white nationalists in the Piney Woods town of Jasper, Texas, known as the "Jewel of the Forest" and the Jasper County seat, about an hour's drive north from Beaumont. Byrd's murder received heavy media attention due to its gruesomeness, the publicized investigation, and the subsequent outcry. It resulted, much later, in hate crime legislation, subsumed under the death of a white gay man—the Matthew Shepard Act—passed a decade later, in 2009, during the Obama administration.

James Byrd was dragged for almost two miles behind a pickup truck before being decapitated when his body hit a culvert. News media and subsequent true crime–style accounts of the event created what people have come to call "trauma porn," the spectacle of the death-space for Black Americans. They focused on details, like how the coroners insisted that he was conscious for the dragging, that he had been urinated on by the three murderers beforehand, that they had picked him up to ostensibly give him a ride home but had inexplicably become enraged by his existence, that police tracked the murderers down by locating one of their knives at the crime scene. The engraving on the knife read "Possum," a regional nickname. George Jones was nicknamed Possum. The moniker has something to do with the nature of a person's grin, a quality of self-satisfaction bordering on mania. Barbara Ching said of Jones: "He may have earned his nickname—The Possum—from his facial features, but his habit of feigning incapacitating intoxication in order to avoid unpleasant situations allowed the name to stick."[23] There is a saying in SE Texas that one is "grinnin' like a possum eatin' persimmon." After killing Byrd, the three men dumped his body in front of a Black cemetery in town. The wretched symbols of the scene—rope, culvert, knife, tombstone—grew large and haunted the space of SE Texas, creating a mixture of further racial divide and cohesion, depending on who is telling the story, which has become a regional fable with different morals.

I found, unsurprisingly, that the story of James Byrd Jr. was told to me by older white folks in SE Texas as a hard-luck story whose implications were deeply divided along racial and class lines. For example, anytime I was told the story of James Byrd by a person of color, regardless of age, it usually either began or ended with a statement about how there are places in SE Texas that are off-limits for people of color to visit, such as "I don't stop for gas in Vidor." A young Black man who was bagging groceries at the HEB in Beaumont made this clear to me after he helped me bring a senior's groceries to her vehicle. We were standing in the parking lot, which was rapidly filling with grackles, the ubiquitous opportunist birds that gather at dusk and dawn in parking lots all along the Gulf Coast and as far inland as Austin. He referenced the highway sign that warned Black people of Vidor's sundown town status. There was an unflinching quality in the way he told the story; it seemed, in some sense, to be uncontested—to *speak for itself.*

Beyond purported historical events such as the billboard, the impacts suffered under white supremacist history and the remnants of place's affect are also being contested, sometimes even more so than the events themselves. What this means is that the function of revising history is in the service of revising the present state of feeling—it is in the service of flattening the story of racism in SE Texas to a seamless progression in which pain is suffered and then left behind (a hard-luck story tethered to a moral) so that the present can be a place where Black people in SE Texas no longer have a legitimate reason to be afraid or angry. Recasting the motives of the Confederacy in the Civil War to be non-racist (the most common historical contestation one encounters from white folks in SE Texas) is connected to recharacterizing the present impasse. The James Byrd story as told by a white person had a profoundly different trajectory—one that was somehow even more troubling. This had to do with the emotional fervor that its telling conjured and with the insistence of some of the tellers (of older generations) that the listener agree with them that the event was a terrible shame, committed by "outsiders," and that its result was actually to bring the community together. This urgency of cohesion took precedence over the trauma suffered; it was supposed to put the trauma to rest.

An older white man from Jasper approached me in the health food store where I worked one evening, and we got onto the subject of James Byrd. I felt that the reason the story was told to me how it was had to do with my whiteness, as well as my being an anthropologist and a "collector of stories," a title I created for myself which I felt made people less uncomfortable than "ethnographer" and fit the strange choreography of Texan politesse that had to be traversed in order to get at anything beyond pleasantries with most SE Texans of the boomer generation and older. The man owned a lawn mower repair shop in Jasper, belonged to a popular Baptist church in town, and had experienced a fair amount of hardship. After frankly, almost proudly, admitting to the racist segregationist practices within the history of Baptist churches in Texas, he told me the by-then-familiar story of James Byrd, with the added detail that the crime was committed by three outsiders, not by people from Jasper.[24] It was important to this man that I understand the gravity of this detail: They weren't locals, figures integral to the small-town functions of familiarity. They were interlopers, individuals with diabolical agencies whose function it was to upset the equilibrium of a community. The most important part of this telling of the story came at the end: the man told me that at Byrd's funeral the town had removed the fences separating the white cemetery from the Black cemetery in a gesture meant to be anti-racist. When he told me this part, he became very moved and began to weep openly in the aisle. His wife, who had been perusing nearby, approached with an apologetic smile and led him away, saying something to me about him "getting like this." He kept repeating: "Those people took that fence down, and our community came together." Stories of race, in this sense, have to be tethered to either hopeful futurity or to a warning; they have to either be "given to God," as the older white gentleman had suggested to me, or brought down to earth in a literal warning not to trespass into spaces where your body would be in danger, as the Black teenager in the HEB told me about stopping in Vidor. The navigation of racialized space happens on very different levels. Here, a certain type of whiteness confabulates and mythologizes racial history into a fable that avoids the grim realities at all costs. But there are competing fantasies vying for space here. Some rush headlong into the darkness of the stuck, as I had found with the stories of the landlord and his world.

In Texas (and other parts of the South), when an utterance requires extra attention or reverence, it is followed or prefaced by "I tell you what." It is like saying "I have told you, or I am about to tell you, something which you should pay attention to." It is nearly saying "Here is something with gravity, something you should hear twice." The landlord commonly used "I tell you what," or the shortened "I tell you," when telling stories that had stuck with him and left a mark that he felt was worth absorbing more deeply than you might. "I tell you what" is a motif for the SE Texan ecology as a sticking point, a way of marking the importance of a story's resonance, a marker or guide. It is like "heard dat," but the transmitting mode of accentuating resonance. What the landlord and the ladies in the RV park enacted in their stories was something active. They didn't merely describe, but situated, gestured toward, and performed the elements of their local cultural real. And these resonant stories sometimes described being under the thrall of things beyond one's control: things felt in the air.

Two

The Higher the Hair, the Closer to God

And no marvel, for Satan himself is
transformed into an angel of light.

CORINTHIANS 11:14

"America Bless God"

"His Fire Will Smite"

"God to America: We Need to Talk"

"Forgiveness Is to Swallow When You Want to Spit"

"Abortion Stops a Beating Heart"

"God Forgives but YOU Have to Kneel"

"Hot Enough For Ya? Try Hell"

"Need a Faith Lift?"

"God Sent the Very First Text Message: The Bible!"

LIST OF CHURCH SIGNS SEEN ON HIGHWAY 96 IN SE TEXAS
ON A DRIVE NORTH FROM LUMBERTON TO BROOKLAND

God Is Alive and Well in Texas

Christian churches dot the rural highways and line the main streets of SE
Texas, outnumbered only by the ubiquitous dollar stores. There are small
Baptist and Pentecostal churches, some of them barely more than shacks,
along the country roads plastered with banners that say things like "Sick?
Jesus Has Healed You!!" and massive near-megachurches along the interstate in the Houston style, beige and sandstone with gigantic parking lots
and brand-new stained-glass windows. The Beaumont Roman Catholic

Diocese covers nine counties, and recreation centers and meeting halls in strip malls are transformed into religious spaces. There are outdoor revivals in parking lots and fields. Churchgoing is ingrained into the ordinary of SE Texas in a way that is seamless and yet constantly making itself known. People want to know what church you go to—they ask if they've seen you at church, or if they can plan on seeing you at church. Christianity forms a public here in a forthcoming manner that is not always the case in other regional spaces, and that sense of being publicly religious is important. Bumper stickers let you know the allegiances and beliefs of their car's drivers.

An old pickup I passed on the highway, weighed down with a bed full of old boxes of junk, had a massive bumper sticker that looked custom-made. It was the word "REPENT," in all-caps white lettering above a quotation from the book of Acts, but each letter either contained or was composed by a symbol that represented a group that, it seemed, the driver felt must repent to make it to heaven. The leg of the *R* was the star and crescent of Islam. The first *E*—stabbed through with both gender symbols, the male arrow jutting from the top, and the female cross protruding from the bottom— represented those who are gender fluid. The open section of the *P* contained the Star of David. The second *E* was a crooked peace sign. The *N* was overlaid with a yin/yang symbol. And the *T* was an ankh. The letters were cartoonishly bent and outsized—there was a playfulness to the font that belied the message it contained and its promise of punishment.

This pull between play and seriousness in Texan religiosity has certain precedents. There is a character that has become part of the Texan mythos and signifies the double pull of secular playfulness and Christian gravity: the Church Lady. Her dressed-up, coiffed bouffant aesthetic is based around getting ready to be seen at church, and her slogan is "The higher the hair, the closer to God." There is a striking juxtaposition between the lightness of this campy adage, which seems to play with secularism's aesthetic excesses and artifice, and the predominance of an utter seriousness in much of the Christian practices in SE Texas. There is a co-constitutive relationship to the secular codes and scenes the faithful find themselves simultaneously embedded within and committing "spiritual warfare" against.[1] There is a lightness and humor inherent in a lot of the sloganeering and visual representations of Christian religious practice in SE Texas, and yet embedded within and proximate to these aesthetic forms tend to lurk more serious commitments to faith. The place that many of my informants' stories ended up showed what kinds of intensities a sustained proximate condition can produce: it can leave people caught up in a joyful fervor; it can wrap them up in a shell of paranoid, conspiratorial thinking; or it can leave them lost and reeling. There are those who navigate a precarious space of moral uncertainty, forever circling the question of their soul's fate and where we are all going, and those (like the health food store employees, discussed below) who infuse the very materials of their everyday lives with the presence and power of God, absorbing His power and presence into their bodies in the form of supplements.

As Courtney Handman has pointed out with regard to one of the truisms of anthropological thinking about religion becoming a private matter, per Weberian individualism, "predictions of the public death of religion have been proven wrong in recent years, as fundamentalism of all types— or even just publicly religious people—have emerged as major forces in contemporary life."[2] SE Texas is one of those regions of the United States that shows just how off base the prediction of religion's demise is—and in ways that seem to blur distinctions about where public and private forms of Christian religious worship draw their boundaries. SE Texas is still, very publicly, an intensely Christian place.

The intensities of the Christian evangelical practices that I encountered in SE Texas had as much to do with where your body would be on Sunday as where your soul would be after your death.[3] There was a dual intensity: that of throwing oneself into the materials and embodied practices and fervors of being in church, of prayer and testimony and song, as well as that of agonizing, philosophizing, and arguing over not only the end of one's life, but also the end of all life and the allotment of souls to different versions of the afterlife. In commitments to various versions of Christian eschatology, thinking and talking about how and when the world as we know it would end and the different versions of millennialism (the belief that Jesus Christ will rule for one thousand years prior to the Final Judgment) was a point of serious dedication for many—most especially among the evangelical and Messianic Jewish folks. Catholics generally condemn millennialism and the Catholic Church has released official statements that strongly reject it, but people of different types of Christian faith, including Catholics, at times expressed beliefs in types of millennialism that did not necessarily adhere to the teachings of their sect or church. Usually, schisms in the details of the end times almost always coincided with or complemented the faith of whoever was speaking. Each millenarian story worked out for those who adhered to the teller's faith; the fate of others (as with the discussion of dual-covenant theology, below) was up for debate and enshrouded in mystery. There was a sense of factionalism, but also a hope and belief in the possibility for others to save themselves. Within the church, the different takes on millennialism most commonly referred to the biblical period as the "Great Tribulation," a time of suffering that would end in "the Rapture." There were social hierarchies and the practice of agonizing over whether your church was getting it right or not. It might take up all of your time, as Michael Warner describes in his reflections on growing up Pentecostal and queer and finding common ways of embodying these aesthetics in incommensurable ideological practices.[4] The endless debating and poring over details is both a pleasure and an awe-inspiring obligation. Like the Church Lady, who is both joking and serious about her coiffed proximity to God, there is a composition of feeling that takes place in the Christian fundamentalist endeavor.

Christian millennialism focuses on a passage from the book of Revelation (20:1–6) that describes the descent of an angel to a "bottomless pit" with a chain and key who imprisons Satan for a thousand years. The temporal schema of what and when the millennium is divides believers into different stripes of millennialism. Premillennialism, which prophesies that Christ's second coming will happen before the period of millennial rule, was the predominant version of millennialism I encountered in SE Texas and the one that the larger evangelical churches in the area seemed to espouse. There was an often precariously balanced tension between the metaphorical and literal elements of the doctrines connected to this belief—most notably the instantiation or appearance of "New Earth," the dwelling place of God's chosen after the end-times. The debates over these increasingly blurry boundaries between metaphor and reality foregrounded the intense preoccupation with the fate of the soul. Knowing what timeline your church adhered to was like figuring out a map that gave you directions and a schedule for when to show up. It was being clear on the rules before playing the game.

In SE Texas, the ways entanglements among apparent incommensurabilities proliferate are significantly colored by evangelical rhetoric and practices. These entanglements are present in all of the elements I speak of in this work: in the hard-luck stories about what brought people to God; the reconciliations with illness, natural disaster, and living in a place where debility is the norm; the intensely loaded figuring of sexuality; and being a character in one's own story. My ethnographic encounters with those on the so-called fringes of evangelical practice most markedly illustrated these entanglements, as they show the far-reaching influence, what might be seen as the call or beckoning, of evangelical practice. The feeling of being *in* something that infuses the everyday with a presence or force that is not metaphorical, such as the ability to count oneself among the inhabitants of a New Earth or to receive various spiritual bolsters in the form of supplements and natural foods, kept people connected to each other and to a world they shared. A significant part of this feeling were the practices of interpretation and narrativization as modes of detecting and excavating profound truths, debating their proper meaning, and applying them to the material world. Like storytelling, familiarity with evangelical ways and interpretation of texts is an adherence to a form: it is a display of communicative and analytical competence as well as a spiritual endeavor.[5] And the pull of belonging to a public whose interpretive practices position them at the top of a spiritual hierarchy structures the ground where all kinds of people find themselves.

Tommy's God

I met Tommy sitting around a fire out in the SE Texas Piney Woods. There was a birthday party, and the night had become wild with drinking and stories. Tommy had a quiet, brooding intensity and seemed to be disconnected from the revelry, watching the others with a small grin. Suddenly, his shyness left him, and he began speaking to me unprompted. He told me that usually he gets drunk enough at these parties to get naked and dance around, maybe even jump over the fire. He was a volunteer fireman, lived in a trailer park in the next town, and worked for a large evangelical church as an IT person. He was more or less openly gay and evangelical, and had spent the past few years of his life navigating the precarity of that situation. The church where he worked and attended services was more or less anti-gay; his sexuality was an open secret. People knew, but the topic was generally avoided. Although he wasn't closeted, the stipulation given to him by the head pastor at the church was that he was not to speak of his sexuality and had to avoid any social media posts that might lead people to believe he was gay. At some point, this rule was broken when Tommy posted a status update declaring that he had met someone. His life had been lonely up until that point, he said, and the excitement of finding a partner had overwhelmed him. The church fired him, and this led to a severe bout of depression in which he attempted suicide. Afterward, there was a reconciliation process with the church, apparently under the same stipulations, and he was given his job back. His relationship to God and the church was important enough to him that he returned to this situation. He said his church was what gave his life structure, connected him to others, and kept his faith alive during a time when there was not much else to believe in. His church, in short, presented him with a different way of being and doing whose benefits of sociality and practice seemed, at times, to outweigh the belief that he was living a sinful life.[6] He valued his "direct" relationship with God, attained through prayer and worship. He considered himself a "Bible-believing Christian," a marker of authenticity within a hierarchical scale, as told to me by various self-designated Bible believers.[7]

Among the evangelicals I spoke to in SE Texas, different kinds of Christianity were placed along a spectrum in their dealings with God. Protestants consider any mediation between the worshipper and God to be superfluous.[8] Despite a complicated reality in which various pastors, officials, and church groups of Protestant faiths perform a fair amount of what could arguably be called mediating practices in their Bible studies, sermons, and church services, mediation is considered a specific set of elements of worship and practice that Bible-believing Christians and evangelicals in SE Texas most often identified with Catholicism. They noted, for example, the seven sacraments of the Roman Catholic Church, such as confession (Penance or Reconciliation) and communion (Eucharist), and the structure of priest-led Catholic masses, in which ritualistic movement such as standing, sitting, and kneeling are dictated according to a certain schedule. The Bible belief or literalism present in evangelical churches has become a much more common element of belief across various forms of Christianity in the United States.[9] The rejection of the Bible as a "story" or an "allegory" was a common thread that connected evangelical and Messianic Jews' accounts of their own faith systems and religious practices. The metaphor of a veil or blindfold being removed, which stood for the allegorical interpretation of biblical passages, surfaced variously in my conversations with members of both religions.

Tommy frequented a remote beach just over the Texan border in Louisiana, southeast of Port Arthur, across the wide expanse of Sabine Lake off the Gulf Beach Highway. Looking back north across this expanse, the foreground was dotted with cattle grazing on rough grasses and sedge just before the beach broke, and while background was populate by a blur of oil refineries and gas plants: Chevron Port Arthur, Valero Port Arthur, Sabine Pass LNG (liquefied natural gas). Tommy brought me to the beach on a number of occasions; I never quite got used to the Texan practice of driving one's truck out onto the beach and along the waves, parking it at some safe distance from others and not worrying about the oil and other emissions from one's vehicle leaking into the sand.

There were infrequently others on this beach, save one occasion when a group of locals on four-wheelers came up and asked us for alcohol or cigarettes. We chatted with them briefly, waiting for the moment in which they would identify us as strange. This moment never arrived; they shot off on their four-wheelers, disturbing a flock of avocets in the tall grass and spinning donuts along the beach—leaving in their wake a spiraling and chaotic track. Avocets are wading birds with unlikely upturned, long, slender beaks. The delicacy with which they comb the waters always took me by surprise, in this world of roughness and damnation. Like tickling fire with a feather. It was when the hollering of the four-wheeler crew had just begun to fade under the steady crashing of the waves that Tommy told me that Hell was a real place.

For Tommy and those of his church, Hell is a waiting room governed by its own suspended temporality. Tommy called it "a place of darkness and eternal separation from God—but a temporary place—until the Final Judgment." When I asked him how a place could be both eternal and temporary, both literal and figurative, we got into a prolonged discussion about literalism and the specifics of evangelical Christian eschatology, or the coming of the end times—literalism in this instance being what we understood to be the spectrum of interpretation of scripture from metaphor to reality. Literalism has various definitions, some of which focus on the chain of evidence from God to the believers. In these instances of literalism, God's word was direct inspiration to the Gospel writers, thereby creating a perfect text that is untainted by mediation. "Eternal separation" could be a chamber where you are literally prevented from being with God or a state of mind in which communion with God was held in abeyance; however, depending on one's view of redemption, this separation could be suspended in nearly an instant. This was done by "coming to Jesus, or to God." I asked Tommy what he thought about classical art depictions of Hell as a fiery torture chamber, to which he replied:

As our church teaches, both Heaven and Hell are technically temporary; they're holding places for souls until the Final Judgment. At the Final Judgment, then, people will be separated, either with God or without God, basically whether you accepted Christ or whether you didn't. At that time, well,

Hell will be cast into the Lake of Fire, Heaven will be done away with, and we will live on the New Earth. Uh, the Earth will be destroyed and remade, uh, out of Revelation, which is an interesting book. New Earth is described, um—best that I can understand it—is described as a place without water, so you have the complete volume of the Earth to live on. Uh, the New City, the New Jerusalem, is basically a cube almost. It's 1,500 miles by 1,500 miles by 1,500 miles, which would actually put it into space, because space is only like 60–70 miles up, so . . . it is described as Paradise, it is described as having fruits to eat from the Tree of Life, there's a lot of descriptions, but bodies of water, as far as I understand it, no. There is a scripture, I don't remember where it is in the New Testament . . . but basically, the Old Testament is a shadow of Christ—all the prophecies that refer to him, um, the Bible talks about the Jews being, not blinded but just—not having the full revelation of what was in their future. Um, as a Christian we can look back on those scriptures and see how they relate to the New Testament. The way I see, the Book of Revelation is our future, so we don't have a full understanding of it. It's a book of prophecy in the same way the Old Testament was to the Jews, the Book of Revelation is to Christians, that's how I kinda see it.

Using Judaism to hierarchically position Tommy's church's version of the New Covenant in Christ is a type of supersessionism (or replacement theology) in which Christians supersede the Mosaic Covenant of the Jews. Generally, the evangelicals and Messianic Jews I spoke to in SE Texas did not speak of Jewish people much outside of these theological boundaries. For many Jewish people, supersessionism amounts to anti-Semitism. A few folks I spoke to even identified anti-Semitism as having waned among Christians in SE Texas over the past few years due to what they saw as the priority of "supporting Israel." I asked Tommy whether he thinks Jews will be welcome on New Earth, to which he replied:

[There is an] enormous amount of debate in dual covenant theology about whether because they are Jews they will automatically be saved or whether they have to accept Christ. Jesus was a Jew, he came for the Jews, the Jews rejected him, so the ministry went out to the Gentiles. Which, there were some Jews that were saved and there are some Jews that still are saved, some of them refer to themselves as Messianic Jews, Jews that believe in Jesus. So there's a lot of different viewpoints— Revelation talks about the 144,000 that will be saved, so there's kinda a lot of hints about it.

God's Food

I became familiar with Messianic Judaism through my part-time job in the supplements department of a health food store (at the time, the only one in the region) in one of the Golden Triangle cities. A short time after starting there, the employees began to ask me about my background, my religious beliefs, and (when they learned of my relatively safe and approachable secularism and my unoriginal joke of being a "recovering Catholic") my interest in learning about their religion. As it turned out, a number of them were Messianic Jews. Although other faiths were represented at the health food store, Messianic Judaism was discussed the most, and forms of proselytization relating to it were the most common. What was interesting about this were the basic similarities with other forms of proselytization I had experienced in SE Texas and elsewhere, the by now familiar "Have you heard about Jesus's plan for you?" style of spreading the word. Because this centering of Jesus dominated the rhetoric, it was significant when I began hearing other employees refer to their proselytizing coworkers as Jews. I came to understand that Messianic Judaism employs stylistic forms strongly undergirded by evangelical Christianity and its speech genres, one of which was strongly influenced by the "interactional frame" of revelation that also influenced the employees' beliefs about supplements and their sales practices and strategies.[10]

The level of proselytization differed depending on whom I was speaking with—Miss Polly and her husband, Patrick, were always keen to discuss their beliefs as Messianic Jews with me, but they never went so far as to invite me to a meeting. Another woman, Myra, who was a massage therapist and a former employee of the store who visited on occasion as a customer and seemed to pick up odd shifts in the kitchen (where the ready-to-eat foods were prepared), was keen to discuss her beliefs and also repeatedly encouraged me to attend Messianic Jewish meetings. These encouragements took place both in the store and at Myra's home, where I once received a massage from her for back pain in a room whose walls were plastered in Jesus collages. Once I was on the table, Myra gently reminded me about Jesus's plan for us all. She was never aggressive or judgmental, and I deflected by speaking of my confirmation in the Catholic Church and my family's relative atheism. I later learned that Messianic Judaism's proselytization practices tend to focus on Jewish people, although I never heard the Messianic Jews at the health food store refer to Jews in any concrete way, either as potential converts or as sinners. I also learned that the Messianic

Jews at the health food store were comfortable in conceiving of their faith as a form of Christianity, which is not necessarily the norm among other Messianic Jews. In fact, a debate about its relation to Judaism has been the focus of much media coverage on Messianic Judaism's presence in Israel, where Israeli Jews have occasionally clashed with them.

During my time at the health food store, I learned that Messianic Judaism is a syncretic religious practice whose modern incarnation was established during the 1960s and 1970s, combining elements of Christianity and Judaism. Previously, I had heard of "Jews for Jesus," which is a branch of Messianic Judaism but is not an interchangeable term for Messianic Jews. It has a small but zealous following in SE Texas. Messianic Jews believe that Jesus (or Yeshua, the Aramaic version of his name, which I heard believers refer to him as occasionally) is the Messiah, and insist that accepting this fact is the only way to salvation. Salvation was referred to using different terms, most commonly through the language of rebirth or spiritual rebirth, with the goal of this process being "reconciliation to God." However, Messianic Jews observe some Jewish rites and holidays, and place special emphasis on the importance of the Hebrew language in unlocking the path to salvation. Miss Polly, the supplements manager at the store, described these syncretic practices as "interference." It was like jamming the signal in order to get at the truth hidden underneath, or optimizing the combined messages of different faiths, mixing all the useful parts together to come up with the best version. She explained to me that she left the Southern Baptist faith because, despite its encouragement of worshipers to develop a direct relationship with God, it didn't go far enough. She told me that certain events described in the Bible were not given enough seriousness and gravity in Baptist sermons. There was a literal description of events taking place, she said, that was being changed into metaphor. She said that the only way to truly reach the "truth" of the Bible was through Hebrew; this was the first description I was given of Messianic Judaism as a hybrid practice that valorized Hebrew as a "power language" that contains both linguistic and mathematical messages for those who study it. One of the things she repeated was that "language is a program," and when another employee asked her what this meant, she clarified:

> In one of my books at home, there, um . . . at one time there was this study they did with semantics, and they had this piece of equipment, um, that they spoke through that amplified the sound, kinda like a trumpet, and at the bottom of it was this dish of sand. And they could speak

and amplify the sound and it would make the sand move. Everybody un-derstands that, when you hear a boombox, um—a loud car go down the road, you hear it, you feel it, so you're feeling the frequencies. So they did different languages through this, um . . . and in the book it says that every language would make the sand move, but when they spoke Hebrew [the movement] was *organized*, it actually formed the letters. So I'm thinkin', if you think of the words as a program, it's sound. It moves things. So it would make sense that Hebrew would be the language that He created with, you know? You speak a word, *it is*. Program the right frequencies, it causes a physical manifestation of what has been spoken, if you've got organized matter that comes together, you know? Isn't that awesome? But you can imagine the looks of things if it was chaos and a word or an organ-ization or a thought, a plan or mathematical equation is sounded, and it all comes into place.

Miss Rudy laughed in agreement and said that is what Hell must look like. This vision of a place evoked in total chaos, without words, without the ability to achieve representation, that is, what is sensible, did in fact seem terrifying.

For Miss Polly and the other Messianic Jews, Hebrew enacts the foun-dational qualities of a worlding, "an incitement to form" in its very utter-ance.[11] The Messianic Jewish interpretation of the supposed experiment carried out on sand requires the biblical quote "In the beginning was the Word" to be understood literally. That is, it would require us to acknowl-edge a definition of the Word in which it is not a way of being or a collec-tion of God's intentions (as the "Word of God" was defined for us in the CCD classes I took as a young Catholic), but it is the actual utterance of words by God himself. Meaning that Hebrew, being as it is the creative power of the universe, could not possibly have been created by God as it was used to initiate the process of creation. Instead, Hebrew must be integral to God's being. This is an idea that goes against the canonical and paradoxical definitions of being proposed in philosophy by figures such as Arthur Schopenhauer, who wrote that "it is true that space is only in my head; but empirically my head is in space."[12] Space is not a concept; it is a manifestation of an utterance. In Miss Polly's interpretation of the sand experiment, language does not distort or abstract the empirical value of lived reality: it literally creates it. Or, at least, Hebrew does.

This literal interpretation of language as a power source that renders and manipulates matter seemed to be a form of deeply held belief with a literature that purported to prove it. What was interesting about the Messianic Jews was that their investment in this unseen or untapped potentiality did not stop at the level of faith—it burrowed deep into the possibilities of manifesting this unseen world through experimentation, exploration, and literal excavation. Miss Polly sent me links to YouTube videos about "Paleo-Hebrew," a way of reading each character of the Hebrew alphabet as a unit containing potentialities that was described in a series of lectures by an archaeologist who Miss Polly said was ousted from the academia when he "revealed" that the events described in the book of Exodus actually occurred and that there was a corresponding archaeological record to support this claim. Miss Polly said, "Somewhere out there, in the desert, there are layers of remains that point to the Plagues of Egypt. Imagine that, knowing that that stuff is out there and covering it up." She was also interested in music that was composed in the "Key of David," music that was supposedly composed in the key that David (of the David and Goliath story from the book of Samuel) used to compose the Psalms. The health food store sold a set of CDs titled *Wholetones: The Healing Frequency Music Project* by a musician/composer named Michael Tyrrell, which Miss Polly played regularly.[13] She claimed that each track (which were all exactly twenty-two minutes and twenty-two seconds long) contained a frequency that healed a different condition, such as liver issues, emotional distress, and so forth. She also claimed that Tyrrell advised to begin with the first track, which would "open one's heart to the healing frequencies." The belief was that in the time of David (ca. 1,000 BCE), music was composed in this key; when modern tuning practices were invented, music lost its inherent healing frequencies. Miss Polly said that the modern practices emerged during the reign of Pope St. Gregory the Great; she believed that the invention of certain instruments, including the harpsichord, required a different key to be invented. Miss Polly also repeatedly stated that the songs on the *Wholetones* CDs were in a different "hertz," or unit of frequency, that she believed was a restoration to the Key of David musical form. Music had stopped having an inherent healing power after it was corrupted, but Michael Tyrrell had restored it to its healing power.

The story that proved this claim, which I took to be a testimonial that was possibly taken from the booklet (that I never saw), was told to a group of supplements employees, including myself, by Miss Polly in the car on the way to a talk given by a well-known naturopathic physician in Houston. She was playing one of the CDs for us while she told the story:

Anyway, so he developed this music around these tones, and meanwhile his mother is in the hospital with cancer, she has a tumor, a pancreatic tumor, and they're fixin' to, um, do surgery to have it removed. So he goes to the hospital right before her surgery, and he goes, "Mother, I feel led to play this music—do you mind?" And she said, "No, go for it," you know? So he rests his guitar, I think, *on* her. And he begins to play this music. And she shuts her eyes, and she starts to see like a big ol' black blob or something leaving. And when it's finally gone, it's just bright green, you know? And then she falls asleep. Next thing you know, they're comin' in to wheel her out for surgery, and they get into the room where they're doin' the surgery, open her up, and it's gone, totally gone. So that was with the music you're hearing right now.

At this point, the store manager, Jill, who was accompanying us on the trip to Houston, interrupted Miss Polly. Jill seemed nervous about continuing the story, as it seemed to have some secret element to it, but allowed Miss Polly to continue to tell us as long as we were discreet. The secret part of the story was that Michael Tyrrell's music was played in the herb garden of the CEO of one of the largest herbal supplements companies in the United States, implying somehow that the herbs were all infused with the Key of David and, therefore, with the precise frequency of the healing power of the music of God. For the employees in the van with me who gasped with delight, this signified a literalizing of the phrase "God's food" in a way that further adhered them to the connecting belief structures in the store. Jill finished the story by saying "They've got to be on that same belief system of frequencies and energy and healing, otherwise you'll sabotage your crop."

Michael Tyrrell's supposedly ancient tuning methods to find a key "between the other keys," as Miss Polly put it, regained the Wholetones' ancient frequencies, pitched by the booklet as lost until now. This method resonated with Messianic Jews like Miss Polly due to their already being invested in methods of Hebrew transposition, such as alphanumeric coding systems like gematria. Gematria is considered by some to have two forms, a "revealed" form that is traditionally a hermeneutic rabbinic practice with roots in the Mishnah (the first part of the Talmud), and a "mystical" form that is associated with the Kabbalah and Kabbalistic practice.[14] Gematria, although I never heard it referred to this way by the Messianic Jews at the store, has been co-opted and used by Messianic Jews in alphanumeric interpretations of the New Testament.[15] Miss Polly explained further:

Numbers are very significant, you know? Michael, we found out, made each one of his songs twenty-two minutes, twenty-two seconds. So, we're studying the letters, and the other day, we had been encouraged to start with each letter of the dictionary and just learn how the words flow together 'cos you could take—in Hebrew, no matter where you are on the word, the whole word is significant. That's why it's so hard to do any kind of translation, you can't just use one word and convey the whole meaning of what's goin' on. So, um, every two letters means something—it's like deciphering the heart of words, you know? So each letter has significance that brings meaning to the word, every two letters have meaning, you know, every three letters—and if you look at it backwards too, and you can see another perspective of what that word means. It's awesome—it's like DNA.

Miss Polly and her husband, as well as all of the other Messianic Jews I met in SE Texas, were not raised Jewish, nor were they ethnically Jewish. This was a point that they themselves often made in order to demonstrate the strength of Hebrew's pull: it had reached all the way into the heartland of Baptist/Evangelist SE Texas. The only synagogue in Beaumont is a Reform Jewish synagogue that, according to another Messianic Jewish woman I met, "preached liberal propaganda." The Messianic Jews did not attend synagogue, finding the core principles of Judaism to be essentially blasphemous (although they did not refer to them explicitly as blasphemy). However, they readily performed Judaic rituals under the proviso that the rituals conformed to the standards of Messianic Judaism, which reinstates Jesus as the prophet while placing emphasis on the reading and teaching of Old Testament (or Hebrew Bible) scripture.

Music and archaeology were two instances in which followers of Messianic Judaism felt that either secularism or other faith systems had somehow corrupted a fundamental "truth" by co-opting its form of production. For Messianic Jews, the co-opting either was done in the service of a corrupt, profit-driven capitalism or was a blasphemous religious appropriation. Rather than calling such co-opting blasphemy outright, however, they contended that the effects of the co-option spoke for themselves, functionally altering the original effects of the "pure" or "literal" phenomenon for the worse through corruption and metaphorization/abstraction.

The connections between political-ideological belief and spiritual practice became more clear in these types of statements, as most of the Messianic Jews I met were, in some form or another, (usually right-wing) libertarians. There was an appeal to the senses of both political and spiritual autonomy, a lack of mediation between the worshipper and God, that mirrored the desire for a lack of interference between the State and the citizen's God-given freedoms. There was also a profoundly held belief in various conspiracy theories about far-ranging topics, from food supply to 9/11, that was mirrored in the conspiratorial elements of Messianic Judaism, which insist that certain spiritual "truths" are being obfuscated by mainline Judeo-Christian religious practice, in some cases deliberately as an attempt to mislead the masses. There was overlap between these spiritual and political beliefs and the community that shopped and worked at the health food store. Messianic Judaism, right-wing libertarianism, and wellness stuck together in the ragtag group of employees and customers.

One common strategy among the three salesladies in the supplements department at the health food store was the expertise with which they insinuated themselves into the hard-luck story of the customer, weaving their own experiences of hardship into the sale. It was a method of connecting to the suffering consumer, but also a crafty way of navigating certain legal and ethical limitations that are placed on their industry. Most notably, these stories told by the ladies take the form of circumventing DSHEA (Dietary Supplement Health and Education Act of 1994), which allows the FDA to regulate supplements. I was brought into the ongoing struggle against and paranoia toward DSHEA (pronounced "D'Shay" by the folks at the store) when I was still in my first week there. I had noticed that many customers asked for Miss Celeste by name. Miss Celeste was the senior salesperson and seemed to have an answer for everything. I answered the phone, and the customer asked for her. I turned to her and said playfully, "Paging Dr. Celeste!" She looked at me down the front of her glasses with horror and took the call. Afterward, she explained that no one should hear me calling her that because it is "against DSHEA, and we can get into a lot of trouble for that."

The DSHEA statute requires, among other things such as clear labeling, that no salesperson of supplements diagnose consumers, speak with medical authority, or imply that a product can cure or treat symptoms of illness in any way. The sales methods of the ladies in the store are effective indicators of the divergent narratives of self-care, illness, and suffering between the world of supplements, broadly described as "alternative medicine," and the medical industry, often referred to at the health food store as "Big Pharma" or "Big Medicine."[16] Although DSHEA's requirements are seen by the employees of the health food store as a tyrannical ruling by the medical industry, many critics of DSHEA actually come from positions of authority within the FDA (albeit from the perspective that it gives the supplements industry too much freedom), such as former commissioner David Kessler, who argued that the regulations allowed the supplements market free rein to sell what it wished so long as it followed DSHEA guidelines. According to Kessler and others within the mainstream medical authority, many supplements are not only ineffective but also dangerous. The conflict between the supplements industry and mainstream medicine has a complicated history, but suffice it to say that the employees and many of the customers at the health food store disagreed with Kessler and his colleagues' position— often citing the multiple dangers of pharmaceutical prescription drugs and the methods of medical doctors. Miss Celeste's oft-repeated adage was that the only recourse of medical doctors is to "burn, cut, and poison." This trifecta of medieval methods was brought forward whenever a question arose as to the efficacy of alternative medicine. Warnings against the tried-and-failed methods of medical doctors were a common strategy: They can "only" radiate, they are monomaniacal and fixated in their treatments, and theirs is at best an arcane and experimental practice. It is profit-based, not care-based. They "treat the illness, not the person." These statements provided an underpinning for the advocacy of holistic medicinal and treatment approaches, and connected alternative and holistic medicinal practices to larger political beliefs. Most significantly, they opened a space in which the Messianic Jews' pragmatic spirituality played a large part in circumventing the oppressive logics of the food and medical industries by connecting them to the idea of the blindfolded, secularist state at large and its practices of hiding the truth of nutrition ("God's food," as it was most often called at the store) from the starving, spiritually and nutrient-wise, masses. "God's food" meant supplements that lacked "isolates" and were made from sprouted and fermented food so that the nutrients were totally "bio-available."

These elements of Messianic Judaism's belief structure coincide with current right-wing libertarian talking points, which are themselves connected to core ideological elements of right-wing libertarianism in the United States. One of the main talking points, as mentioned previously in the supersessionism discussion, was support of Israel's continuing occupation of Palestine as a centerpiece for discussing what they call replacement theology: the Christian belief that the Church has replaced the Israelites as the chosen people of God as well as anti-Islamic rhetoric in its connection to conspiracies about former president Barack Obama and his ties to the Middle East, ISIS, and liberalism's more general connections to and supposed support of "Islamist" terrorism. These beliefs manifest in various far-reaching conspiracy theories about George Soros and the Clinton family's control of the Democratic Left, foreign affairs, and foreign investments and underhanded business deals. Libertarianism's more general attachments to sovereignty also work well with the underlying framework of Messianic Judaism. Regular customers who were not Messianic Jews themselves often found common ground in conversations that began with basic assertions of a desire for autonomy. One of these customers was Poodle, a friend's aunt who sent me daily emails from right-wing libertarian sites and made a lot of her own substances at home, such as essential oils and colloidal silver.

Politesse and Paranoia

Poodle and her husband went to Idaho in the early 1990s to join James "Bo" Gritz's constitutional covenant militia/survivalist movement. They bought and gutted an old school bus, filled it with their belongings, and left SE Texas for colder climes. Their destination was Almost Heaven, a compound that Gritz had settled in Woodland, a Quaker community north of Kamiah, Idaho. They told me that "at one time, it was the most advertised subdivision in the world." They disliked the terms "commune" and "cult." They built several straw bale houses ("rats and woodpeckers love 'em," said Poodle's husband), earthships (houses made from rubber tires), and rammed-earth homes. The place was billed as outside the purview of government control, a utopia where residents could be truly free. They enjoyed the company of their like-minded neighbors and lived off the land. But the stuck finds its way into even the most seamless arrangements. Gritz, speaking to a journalist years after the disbandment of the compound, referred to some of its troublemakers as "knots" who ended up bringing about its demise.[17] These folks allegedly took the compound's anti-government stance a bit too far for Gritz's taste—plotting to murder a judge and blow up propane-tank farms; they even renounced their US citizenship as "sovereigns of the Idaho State Republic."

It is pertinent to describe the groundwork upon which these interactions in the health food store took place in order to understand the sense of delicacy with which these views were expressed, through tact and subtlety, with occasional emotional outbursts. In Texas, there is a widely circulating notion that Texans are polite. However, although it is true that something like a Texan civility does circulate among people, there are also a number of qualities about this politesse that make the statement "Texans are polite" an oversimplification. It is the reason that you might speak of Texan politesse instead of merely American politesse. There is a peculiar regionalism to it. It is a comfort and a refuge for those acting within its strictures, as well as a social lubricant. At the same time, it can fall into the binding of representation—it stands for ugly feelings and ideas, it "means" that something untoward is being hidden beneath the smiles. The pause, the drawl, the drawn-out aside, the artful manner in which a story begins that relates maybe only vaguely to the matter at hand—these gestures can and are often reduced merely to stupidity, to willful ignorance, backwardness. However, this reduction flattens the capaciousness of Texan sociality to the level of backward rhetoric, when it is actually a repertoire of social maneuvers—an arsenal of "bless your heart" styles.

Greeting customers at the health food store was an exercise in the delicate subtleties of Texan politesse. A balance of etiquette and, if the opening was provided, an exercise in which sarcasm and humor are executed with skill. The cashiers were required to greet customers at the entrance, usually with some variation of "How're y'all today?" This would be met with a variety of ebullient wisecracks. One old fellow hobbled in with the response: "If I were doin' any better, I couldn't stand it." An old wealthy lady who was a regular liked to respond with "Well, I was doin' real good 'til I came in here!" accompanied by a smile and a wink. She used a walker on wheels that had a bag built into it where she placed her groceries. She moved very slowly and with a lot of dignity. The double meaning of the joke was that she was regretfully spending her money and yet the quality of the store compelled her to do so—this made the joke also a compliment.

There was a way in which older customers presented themselves to the supplement department, as if to say, "I have lived hard and I have mistreated myself and I am hurting—I submit to your authority." There was a practiced, confessional air about it—a manner of approaching with a slackening suspicion, slowly beginning to hear the supplements representative's words after they had made their ailments known. It often happened in this way: A supplements representative would be standing either at the computer or the shelves, their back turned to the entrance. The customers approached and made themselves known, often without an introduction—"I need somethin' for this gout," for instance. Depending on the representative, some variation of efficiency and accommodation would be put forward. Miss Celeste (who was also a practicing Messianic Jew) would very slowly turn and look over her glasses, which she wore down far on the bridge of her nose. She would assess the customer and then spin toward the appropriate product, her broomstick skirt twirling. She wore "nothing with a waistband"; there was some mysterious reason for it, a growth of some sort on her torso. Or else she would continue to stock the shelves unbothered, finishing her task before leading the customer to what they were looking for. It seemed to depend on the time of day and how she was approached, brusquely or with some show of deference.

Miss Rudie, a devout Catholic, was more conspiratorial and direct. She would turn fully to the customer at once and place her hands behind her back, her face becoming thoughtful. The feeling conveyed was that she was thinking this through together with the customer somehow. Her brow would furrow, and she often looked heavenward as she tapped her mouth in thought. She would begin to nod: "Yes, I've heard of that." She would become gregarious, applying a New Orleans charm. She was the Louisiana Egg Queen in her younger days, a pageant connected to the Louisiana Farm Bureau.

Miss Bertha (who identified as either Pagan or Wiccan in different circumstances—a worrisome idea to the others, yet not without some overlap in belief) would often ask whether the customer has considered some other, more useful or effective, item. She would stand erect and attentive, and weigh options with her hands out, gesturing pros and cons. She referred wistfully to the store she used to work at in Ohio; things were done differently there.

It only took a turn of phrase, an effective show of pain, for any of the salesladies to cry. This was often done with the customers—cracks opening in the tenuous shell of civility and getting at the core of life, crying together as mutual exposure.

All three of the ladies in supplements had led difficult lives. They had grown children in prison or on drugs, had all experienced occasional homelessness and displacement from eviction or hurricanes, had suffered the loss of loved ones due to sickness or to bad, irreconcilable beliefs. They drove many miles to visit their families in uncomfortable homes or in prison, often sleeping in their cars and vans; they received emails and letters from them asking for money, or receive emails from other people whom they don't know in connection to something illegal their child has done. They led precarious lives, paycheck to paycheck, relying on support from friends or acquaintances from their churches or from their addiction support groups. They lived in other people's homes or barely held onto their own, and they often took care of others: neighbors, fellow parishioners, and near-strangers all benefited from their kindnesses.

During my time at the store, I watched the ladies infuse their performance of product sales with these experiences in a way that was very different to any form of "customer service" I had previously encountered, where personal lives were meant to be kept out of sight at all costs and a totally different presentation of self was required. Here, a wounded life, the hard-luck life of the scarred warrior, was expected, if not exactly encouraged, by the management, who viewed the ladies' crying and hard-luck stories with a condescending tolerance. The crying became an endpoint in the ritual of the sale, meaning that the ladies all seemed to perform the act of the sale up until the moment of weeping, at which point they allowed the feeling to take them and the labor of attempting to actually sell anything was abandoned. Miss Celeste cried the least often. At first, their crying struck me as insincere; I cynically felt that there was something of the televangelist in it, the Tammy Faye Bakker or Jan Crouch performance. Until I looked closer at the hard luck that had befallen them and brought them to this place of mutual suffering, I wasn't able to concede that any aspect of this process could be genuinely felt. The salesladies' hard-luck stories that they used in sales paralleled each of their own stories of how they came to their respective faiths.

Logically, they gained nothing from the crying; it couldn't have been beneficial to them as a sales strategy as there was no sales commission system, and the pay was barely above minimum wage. The crying often led to a brief embrace, the rubbing of a back, or, in more rare circumstances, prayer. The sales representatives usually led these prayer moments, although there were exceptions. The prayers were nondenominational in the sense that the faiths of those involved were more often than not mixed, and so their structure was in some way generalized. They were given a devotional air that seemed suitable for the occasion due to brevity. Miss Rudy, after telling a customer that she would like to pray with them, would close her eyes, turn her face heavenward, and pray: "Dear God, we pray to you today that Mrs. Alderson finds a little bit of peace and a little bit of hope with these herbs, and we pray to you to help her husband in his time of trouble, Amen." Everyone else would say Amen, Miss Rudy would silently make the sign of the Cross, and the impromptu prayer group would disperse with hugs.

Miss Bertha's pagan/Wicca beliefs were a taboo subject, broached only when she wasn't present unless she herself brought them up, in which case they were met with polite nods and very little commentary. In her absence, her beliefs were discussed briefly as a shocking peccadillo and an anomaly. However, on a number of occasions when Miss Bertha would speak of performing pagan rituals or spells, the others took interest and even contributed their own anecdotes. It became clear that one of the primary ways in which the apparently incommensurable spiritual beliefs of the ladies in supplements converged was through spirits, sometimes also called demons—both as ever-present guides and protectors that live both inside and outside the bodies of human beings, and as antagonistic, malevolent presences that are able to be manipulated (summoned, banished, sealed in, sealed out, etc.) through ritualistic movement or recitation. These manipulations were, depending on who is speaking, referred to as rituals, cleanses, prayers, or spells. I overheard Miss Celeste telling one of the other salespeople that her daughter had asked her to cleanse her home of bad spirits, which were somehow dwelling there, uninvited. They were upsetting objects in her daughter's house and causing a general ill feeling. She described performing a "sealing ritual," in which she burned various sages in order to protect the home from an unnamed male spirit. She said:

> And the house was all closed up, and I started at the doors and worked up, opened the doors, start at the top and go down, because I didn't tell her, but weeks later I'm down here again, and I'm on the phone talking to her, and she says, "Mom, it's the craziest thing." She says, "I'll be sittin' down here and somethin', a picture will just fly off the wall and hit the other wall," and just, you know, a buncha stuff like that, and I went [*gasps*], "I locked him in instead of out!" [*laughs*]

It was also via the shared commitment to spells/rituals that the ladies in supplements universalized their spiritual experiences and practices—meaning that in each instance of a spell or ritual being discussed, an opening emerged in which to position themselves and one another as fundamentally spiritual practitioners. This was a strategy for asserting solidarity regardless of their methods for achieving a connection to their respective deities. This was especially made clear in their commitments to prayer, in which what was asserted was the importance of making oneself a "conduit" to God, regardless of one's path toward that connection. Sometimes they referred to themselves as prayer warriors or spiritual warriors, regardless of faith, and maintained a basic politesse and respectful tone toward one another while discussing their respective spiritual practices. Going back to superstition as a profound investment, François Bonnet notes:

Superstition is a modality of being-in-the-world. It is not an ad-hoc string-ing together of more-or-less justified, more-or-less grounded beliefs, a ro-sary of faithless explanations. On the contrary, it is a tendency to believe that the world is irrigated by invisible forces, emerging and dissipating to the rhythm of ritual gestures and fortuitous coincidences. What this implies, ul-timately, is that the world possesses an obscure side, which casts its invisible glimmer on the real, but whose interventions are knowable and avoidable—in short, it implies that an economy of the invisible is possible.[18]

Indeed, the ladies also came together on the question of objects, sub-stances, and products sold in the supplements department holding great medical and spiritual power. This was most often understood as the objects or substances being infused with the healing power of God, or, in rarer times, an unknown (almost paranormal) spiritual heft. This infusion was understood to be superior to "chemical" or "laboratory-made" power, and was often characterized as raw, natural, real, or, in the case of ingestible products, containing "God's food." This was a repurposing of marketing strategy that was vastly different than any I had seen in natural foods or organic market settings up until that point—sales representatives con-necting the marketing language of the natural foods industry directly to Judeo-Christian spiritual belief, infusing what is usually peddled as secu-larist/non-Western spiritualist/liberal consumerist practices with a differ-ent ideological and spiritual bent. This was a somewhat novel collision of what are often taken to be opposing ideological practices.

It is difficult to find reliable or unbiased sources to support or debunk the claims made by these products, as most people look to internet sources that end up being extremely biased for or against the product without presenting verifiable evidence. Both "sides," for and against supplements in general, have inbuilt presuppositions that position their views as either author-itative (in the case of those on the side of "science") or under duress. This latter position, used by those in the store and by advocates of supplements more widely, contends that their enterprise operates under the shadow of Big Business, Big Pharma, a cast of "big" entities that dictate, distort, and obscure the reality of the benefits of natural foods and supplements (as well as a whole host of other elements of life that add up to a feeling that modernity is a vastly planned falsehood or blindfold). If I were to cite a medical or scientific study that debunked a supplement, the canned re-sponse would be to inquire "who was funding" the study or in whose ser-vice the study was conducted—questions that, in the end, seemed both valid and only answerable up to a point. The gist of these arguments was that it was difficult to know the truth when the truth was dictated by the powers that be, a shadowy conglomerate of forces that could never be named or exposed by virtue of their nearly limitless power. This narrative tended to fit well with the already widespread beliefs surrounding truth, government, and the existence of vast conspiracies constituting SE Texas's conservative political and spiritual atmospheres, whereas in other regions of the United States where I had previously encountered such ideas, these inbuilt presuppositions were most commonly identified with liberal "new age" or "hippie" spiritualism. This reversed the purview of who were the established powers, who were the blind rabble (the "sheep" or "sheeple," as they were sometimes called), and who were the enlightened resisters.

Products such as bentonite clay, colloidal silver, and marine phytoplankton were characterized, especially by Miss Celeste, as heal-alls: "raw and natural" substances that, if applied to the skin or ingested, could ameliorate or even cure a vast range of medical issues. To avoid using the language of curing, these products were sold with the implication that they were infused with a natural or spiritual healing power. The sale of these products had a surprising success in a little health food store in a corner of Texas certainly not known for its health. There were sections at the ends of aisles designed to draw attention to certain products, "end caps" in retail language, devoted to these products like small altars. Salespeople and customers would gather around them, regaling one another with anecdotes about healing an abscess by rubbing it with clay, banishing respiratory illness by ingesting colloidal silver through the nose, or curing cancer by taking phytoplankton daily in a dropper. And then the hype around a particular product would pass, and it would hardly sell at all for weeks. There was a product called Garcinia cambogia, a supposed weight-loss supplement derived from Malabar tamarind fruit, that was the subject of an article by Dr. Oz. It sold very well for several weeks after the article was published; a month later, it hardly sold at all.

Although the ladies never explicitly admitted to using a spiritual framework for selling products, the feeling that the ladies in the supplements department conjured when peddling these products seemed to be spiritual. What was being evoked was an ahistorical biblical scene in which "ancient people" culled natural remedies from the earth, pregnant women ingested clay from sacred rivers, food was untainted by the stain of industry, and the bounty of Nature was unfettered. This scene, both romantic and somehow in collusion with fundamentalist, nationalist ideas of American selfhood, sometimes brought tears to people's eyes. It evoked a vision that affected them profoundly and truly made them feel as if by participating in this vision (and therefore becoming consumers of it), they were getting "back" to the truth. The processes through which this epiphany could occur were conveniently found on the shelves of the supplements department and were given spiritual connotations. Detoxification was easily the most prominent of these.

Detoxification is a very commonly used word in the natural foods and supplements world, usually shortened to *detox* or *detoxing*. It was one of the most common words used at the store to describe what products like clay and different types of cleanses do for the body, but it was also suggested that the process had more profound effects—detoxing not only the body, but also the mind and the spirit. Detoxification is ostensibly the process through which the body, with the aid of a product like bentonite clay, rids itself of so-called toxins and returns to a healthy state. These products were especially popular despite the fact that the definition and validity of detoxification has been contested and debunked by medical practitioners who argue that detoxification is not a process that the body undergoes via the ingestion of supplements and that the word *toxins* is incorrect in describing the substances that proponents of substances like bentonite clay are claiming to rid the body of—additionally warning that clay potentially contains dangerous substances like lead. In the case of bentonite, an absorbent aluminum phyllosilicate clay that is sold in various forms including clay, liquid, and powder, the supposed benefits are both internal and external. It can be either rubbed directly onto the skin or ingested. Sales reps in supplements departments pitch the process of detoxification as a physical and spiritual trial in which the body and mind potentially get worse before they get better due to the intensity of toxin removal. Satisfied users of bentonite clay at the store would claim to be free of "toxic" materials, sometimes claimed to be colon lining, which had sloughed off in the detoxification process. Some users shared pictures taken with their phones as proof. The pictures showed a gray, ribbed substance, or lumpy hunks that just appeared to be excreted clay.

Colloidal silver, "a suspension of submicroscopic metallic silver particles in a colloidal base," is taken internally, both in the eyes and through the nose.[19] It was also a bestseller at the store, due to its supposed antimicrobial properties, which could cure or treat practically any disease, from AIDS and cancer to parasites, acne, hemorrhoids, or an enlarged prostate. Poodle made her own colloidal silver and distributed it to her family as a replacement for antibiotics and other pharmaceutical treatments. Various sources have attempted to debunk the benefits of colloidal silver, most sources coming to the consensus that silver in colloidal form is relatively harmless, if ineffective. However, taking it in abundance does seem to cause permanent side effects, such as turning people blue or silver. I didn't believe this until I saw the customer they called the Silver Man, a semi-regular who never shopped in supplements but would get his groceries and produce at the store. He had evidently overused colloidal silver, and his face, hair, and hands were a bright metallic bluish-silver tone due to a buildup of silver oxides on the skin (the condition is called argyria). He was treated with pity by the employees and discussed as a glutton, or lotus-eater, in the mythic sense, having imbibed God's power in an irresponsible way and now bearing the stigmata of overconsumption.

Miss Luann was a church lady in the "the higher the hair, the closer to God" aesthetic sense. She drove down from a small town in Tyler County a few days a week to pick up shifts in the supplements department. She was the most outwardly devout of all the employees at the store, a strict Southern Baptist who attended church multiple times a week. What I mean is that she was the most vocal about and insistent upon her faith, and she spoke about her church services and faith more often than the others did. She regularly told stories about everyday miracles that had occurred in her life or in the lives of those close to her. Often, the structure of the miracle stories was such that the quality of the miraculous was layered, meaning it instantiated blessings in the lives of whomever it was affecting on multiple levels, some of which might not be seen at first. These are hard-luck stories strapped to lights at the ends of tunnels, sometimes dim. Sometimes just "not dying" was the light. Miss Luann once told a story about her cousin's husband who had a mishap while doing yardwork (tractor mishaps are a subgenre of hard-luck story in SE Texas):

Anyway, he was done doin' whatever he was doin', he was on his tractor comin' back home. He got to the gate, and there was this log that had fallen—he wanted to get it out of the way, so he tried pushin' it with his tractor . . . and it was bad. It was a hornet's nest! He got stung two hundred times, from the top of his head to the bottom of his feet, but the only place there was no stings were around his ankles. Everywhere, just stingin' him all over. Well, Loralee, my cousin, ran out there, she could hear him *screaming*. She called 911 and they came—well, she had to get in the car because they live way, way back in the woods, so they wouldn't have been able to find them. So they said, "Well, you just need to go ahead and bring him because we can't find you." She got him in the car, she got stung three or four times, they got him to the hospital and got him whatever he needed. He didn't go into anaphylactic shock. But the thing is: good thing he was awake and could talk, he said, "Baby, you need to go back to the house." He says: "I forgot to turn off the tractor." See, and it would have caught on fire and started a forest fire. So, we're praising God's name because Jim, her husband—he has all kinds of health problems, and he withstood everything. God *sustained* him. God *came through* him.

What was miraculous to Miss Luann and the others who heard this story was not only that Jim survived the hornet attack, but that the chain of events leading to Loralee going back to turn off the tractor was the culmination of a miraculous progression that proved God's intervention on both bodily (sustainment) and phenomenal ("came through") levels. Miss Luann was exuberantly friendly, a divorcee, and like the other ladies had clearly seen troubles. However, unlike them, she was not forthcoming about her past, besides snippets relating to the miracle stories, and would never be found crying with customers. The first miracle story she told me was that her ex-husband had recently won seven million dollars in the lottery. She told me that she was scared for him, because "that kind of money does things to people," and that she prayed for him every night. It was one of the only times she expressed a frank vulnerability and openness about her life (despite being couched in the language of attempting to aid another's soul), usually opting instead for an expertly executed Texan politesse that held the messy potentials of interaction at a safe distance. She was quick with a biblical quote and seemed to have a nearly limitless supply of sunny laughter, which could be in reaction to anything, even things that weren't necessarily funny. This made her a bit daffy to the other ladies, who never quite accepted her into the fold, despite her religious enthusiasm and knowledge of natural remedies. She regularly made mullein tea from plants she foraged in her garden and brought it in to share with the rest of the employees.

It was in overhearing some of Miss Luann's conversations with Patrick, Miss Polly's husband, that it became clear to me that the understanding of value within the health food store's religious community with regard to products was hierarchical and depended on which spiritual practices were connected to the substances or products. Anything associated even remotely with Middle Eastern ethnicities (excluding Israeli, which was given the highest value in terms of region besides the United States) or related to what the employees understood as Islam was considered ineffective, even anti-spiritual or anti-healing, bolstering the Islamophobic beliefs of the majority of employees at the store. Islam was the one spiritual practice that was beyond the pale for the health food store employees, and their political beliefs meshed with their ideas about health, diet, healing, and the very nature of reality to create their hierarchy of religions. Which is to say that, although the store employees' views of Islam, and of Islamic natural remedies, were clearly shaped by their choice of news media, among other factors, they treated the presumed lack of efficacy in Islamic natural remedies as "further evidence" of the overall case for Islam being a bad religion. However, if I were to suggest that their dismissals of Islam were ideological or xenophobic (as I did on a few occasions), my suggestion was rejected. The reason proffered for why Islamic faith practices nullified the healing properties of natural substances while Christian practices augmented them came back to the corruption of the practices of Islam, as well as its apparent status as a religion untethered from any moral universe, which was chiefly proven by its apparent opposition to Judaism and therefore to Hebrew, a literal death sentence for any worldview as it meant the mode of creation, the way of being, was denied or opposed.

One afternoon, an Arabic-speaking couple came in looking for qust, an Arabic word for a plant called *Saussurea costus*. Qust is a species of thistle native to South Asia but cultivated widely in the Middle East and South Asia as a medicinal plant. Normally, when a customer entered the store asking for a product that the employees were not familiar with, everyone would stop what they were doing and gather around the ancient, slow computer to Google the product and learn about it, usually with great enthusiasm. If it was a product that was not carried in the store, the buying manager would often consider ordering it. On this occasion, when the Arabic-speaking customers entered, they were greeted in a bemused fashion by Patrick and soon told that the store did not carry the product and had never heard of it. After they had gone, Patrick had me Google qust and I read the description to him, that it was a plant thought to have medicinal and spiritual properties within the Islamic faith. Patrick scoffed and walked off, saying the word "spiritual" with a contemptuous irony. I read further that qust is actually a medicinal plant considered sacred by many faiths, including Judaism and Christianity; it is variously called kosht, costus, or kuth. However, because the employees' first encounter with the plant was associated with Islam (there was no actual evidence that the couple were Muslim as they had spoken little English and had certainly not asserted any religious belief, but the woman was wearing a kerchief that the employees assumed to be a hijab) was enough to warrant dismissal.

Two regular customers, an ebullient mother and daughter named Pearl and Kristy, visited the store almost daily. They made the drive from Orange, where they lived together and regularly attended an evangelical church a few times a week. They were very public in their religiosity, praising God and repeating such phrases as "God is good every day" or "in Jesus's name" after statements regarding people having sudden turns of good fortune or showing tenacity. They joined the employees and other customers in prayer whenever it occurred; Pearl sometimes led these impromptu prayer circles, and she was often seen imparting various wisdoms, both religious and health-wise, on the other customers. She was an expert storyteller, regaling us with hard-luck stories related to shared faith experiences, such as encountering desperately intense, indigent strangers who had "a particular glow" in their eyes that told the women that person was inexplicably holy or angelic, sent from heaven with some sign. One of the stories was about a transient they encountered in a parking lot whom they first assumed to be threatening. He asked for directions, and when he came closer to them, there was an aura of holy power around him that left them speechless—he had intensely piercing eyes. Pearl and Kristy traded vegan and vegetarian recipes and supplement tips with the Messianic Jewish employees and other customers. They also shared similar political beliefs with the cross-section of libertarian ideology present in the store, once telling me laughingly that a neighbor of theirs in Orange actually wore tinfoil hats. The tinfoil hat has become a mainstay of liberal mockery of right-wing conspiracy theorists and libertarians who allegedly believe that donning a hat made of aluminum foil protects you from government surveillance or having your mind controlled by aliens.

Pearl told me that the neighbor did believe those things and had actually prepared a PowerPoint presentation on tinfoil hats that explained what had led him to this practice. In the end, they said, "it was pretty convincing, actually," and they didn't feel he was so crazy after that. Their belief that we are susceptible to the immaterial and the invisible rang out in his descriptions of electromagnetic waves interfering with the processes of one's mind, which they understood to have a baseline state constituted by pure flow, a state of mind that is natural and open to messages from God. This state of mind was always conceived as a precarious balance, maintained with some difficulty given the impingements of life. Aided by various material and immaterial factors, such as supplements, healthy living, and sharing the ever-vigilant practices of one's faith with others who share in this vigilance, it is possible to reach, or to "return to" that baseline state. It is a state in which you are able to keep the lines clear, as it were, for the messages underneath.

Three.

Queer Character and the Golden Triangle

The Collector of Lost Boys

Crossing the Trinity River on our return to SE Texas from the VA in Houston, the collector turned to me and said: "I get so tired of worrying about my mortality." We had just come from his cardiologist where he had been given some bad news about his heart. He had suffered a heart attack a month previous and expected an uneventful routine follow-up. The collector had been living with HIV for almost three decades, and, as an elder in SE Texas's gay scene, he worried about his physical appearance despite being aware of what he characterized as the pitfalls of vanity associated with gay men. The collector was the director of a political action committee (PAC) in SE Texas that focused on LGBTQ+ rights and lent support to politicians who prioritized such rights. Such activity was no small feat given the political reputation of SE Texas. Besides the city of Beaumont, which the collector described as "locked down blue, thanks to the Black vote," the surrounding rural and suburban areas of the region were infamously conservative and racist. Originally hailing from New England, the collector had been involved in gay rights initiatives in SE Texas since 1994, when he moved there to take care of a partner's ailing mother and ended up staying. Drawn to the self-sufficiency and "roughin' it" mentality of life in SE Texas, the collector was intimately familiar with the affective states of severity that characterize the feeling of life there for many of its inhabitants, both bodily and atmospherically. I met the collector while attempting to track down a contact for the PAC, having been amazed that such an organization would even exist in SE Texas.

The collector lived out in the swamps, at the periphery of one of the backwaters skirting Beaumont. The first time I drove to meet him was a misty, dark SE Texas evening. The low fog mixed with the smoke from the refineries. I passed the Goodyear plant, belching smoke out onto the road that a wind had brought down to ground level. It had the effect of passing through a portal. The collector met me at a local gas station since finding his place would be too difficult on my own, he said. I followed him back to his house, through a small clearing off one of the farm-to-market roads and along a muddy path riven by wheel marks and bordered by swamp grass and cattail. His house stood a few hundred meters back into the woods in a manmade clearing. It stood about fifteen feet off the ground on wooden beams—he had raised the house after one of the hurricanes—with layers of collected junk, tools, and miscellaneous equipment piled underneath it. On the porch patrolled two ancient black Labs, sturdy and gentle and blind. It was very dark, save for the lights emanating from inside the house that cast a dim glow over the surrounds. I realized that I had left my phone at home in the trailer, as I followed the collector through the door and watched him lock a complicated series of door locks, the mechanics of which I tried to quickly memorize.

My fears were soon abated; the collector was incredibly gregarious— he had made a venison gumbo and quickly launched into story after story about his own history, as well as the history of SE Texas since he had arrived some two decades previously. He began almost immediately to tell me about the goings-on of the PAC and the local gossip and drama that in his view prevented the PAC from getting anything done. There was a broader connection that this inefficiency (which he recognized as a gay issue) had to gay community-building more generally. He told me about the many connections he had in the community and beyond, and how helpful he could be for my project. I felt very welcomed, but also recognized a dynamic taking form, on my behalf, which positioned us in a mentorship. He told me he takes younger gay guys who are in need "under his wing." I learned that he was a mentor, spiritual guide, and adviser to a loose-knit local group of mostly gay men around the age of twenty-five, the majority of whom were ex-military, medical workers such as paramedics or EMTs, and volunteer firemen, paid firemen, or police officers. He had organized an LGBTQ+ first-responder unit in Beaumont, and these men had target practice on his property every month or so, firing their guns off in the woods at beer bottles and handmade targets. They were, in his estimation, guys who had lost their way, in the thrall of some toxic relationship with military or local official bureaucracy, or in a contentious relationship with their church, a fire station, or family. Young men who had come back from active duty with PTSD, ostracized by local veterans' groups. The collector invested much of his time in dealing with their troubles, which were sometimes quite serious. He collected lost boys.

This kind of relationship is something that I have observed in gay communities generally, but never with the intensity as I observed in SE Texas. The relationship is deeper than a mentorship, in which the trajectory of the interaction is understood by both parties to be didactic. These relationships are more slippery, sometimes darker, although the collector seemingly never had bad intentions for his mentees. This isn't to say that there wasn't an element of desire to these relations, but that the collector rarely voiced or acted on them. In a place like SE Texas, where finding a sympathetic ear is rare for queer folks, these relationships take on a more high-stakes dynamic—a friend being one's lifeline is a much more common occurrence here.

What all of the collector's stories seemed to have in common was a characterization of himself as a mentor for young gay men who were in trouble. This is why I began to call him the Collector of Lost Boys—a nickname I told him about around a campfire one evening. He chuckled at this name and said to me with some astonishment that he was taken aback by how accurately I had captured what he "does." These were stories of addiction, suicide, illness, depression, and the precarity of barely holding onto a life that was slipping out of one's control. The stories were, like the landlord's world in the trailer park, a catalog of characters. One difference here was that the collector wanted to convey the similarity and intractability of all the stories of the lost boys, while the landlord was more interested in the variety of strange tales. This struck me as a difference between the styles of accrual and array, in which, on the one hand, the poetic heft of the catalog relies on the building up of repetition to show a mounting tension, whereas, on the other, the catalog is meant to dazzle with sharp turns and the assorted visions of American grotesquerie.

The collector told me three hard-luck stories in quick succession that first evening. These were stories that recurred in our conversations; they served as touchstones and entry points into the severity and tragedy of being gay and alone in SE Texas. The first was about a young gay man who lived in total isolation as a shut-in, having been rejected by his family after coming out. He became very ill and had a condition where his legs swelled up to the point where he couldn't move around. The collector ended up taking care of him until his death, and he had marveled at the accumulation of objects and filth in the man's house as a result of his hoarding. His life was a tower of dusty objects stacked up around him. The second story was about a young gay guy who lied about inheriting $8 million; he had a group of people who believed this and stuck around him for this reason. He had health problems related to drugs, and the collector remembered sitting in the hospital room and overhearing these people speculate about what was going to happen to his money after he died. When the collector finally told them that there was no money to inherit—that the man had lied in order to have friends around him—they drifted away, and the man was left alone with the collector. The third story was about a young veteran who became addicted to pain medication and "doctor-shopped," meaning he went from hospital to hospital trying to get doctors to prescribe him medications for exaggerated ailments. He attempted suicide on New Year's Day, and his family called the collector for help. The collector sat in the man's living room with him while he held a gun to his head, and he eventually talked him down. They remained good friends, and the collector considered him one of his few success stories.

Many of the lost boys had experienced serious traumas in family lives around being gay. They shared a wound that brought them together. The hard-luck stories told to me by the collector described a mode of bonding that is not necessarily peculiar to SE Texas or even to rural areas, but it took as its starting point an altogether different LGBTQ+ character who did not presume that "it gets better"; the bond was not tethered to a hopeful futurity or anticipatory vision. There was instead a way in which the wound of being queer in SE Texas was an honorific; it marked its participants as beings who were not separate from the world that caused their pain, but were throwing themselves into life and weathering the storm that this constant endeavor brought.

Queer Rurality

Some recent work on queer rurality recasts the rural United States as space in which queerness thrives despite being unwelcome.[1] This work redeems rural space as inhabitable by showing that phenomena such as "gay migration" are not unidirectional: people don't just leave the country, they come back to it too.[2] When presented with this idea, Bill, a middle-aged gay SE Texan native who was HIV positive, scoffed: "Listen, the main reason gay men of my generation came back to this town was to die—that's why I came back here. I just didn't die." Bill told me that he migrated to the West Coast in the mid-1980s and got into computer science. He was hired by a defense contractor and put through a series of psychological evaluations. The company therapist was the first person he "came out" to, as it were; in order to pass the security clearance and become "unblackmailable," they made him go back home to Beaumont and come out to his Baptist preacher father and mother, whom he described as "leaving the room and never returning." Six months later, he went back home for good and came out to them as HIV positive. Bill's story challenges not only the idea of gay migration as unidirectional; it also troubles the very idea of grouping around a set of politics such as liberationist or queer radical resistance. For Bill, the gay men of SE Texas ended up thrown together under the banner of debility—not through some sense of solidarity. His narrative suggests that while he would rather have lived in the city, the intractable events of his life forced him back into the stuck relations of home. The closet did not function for him as a space of avowal, but was the beginning of a series of events that led to a more troubling terrain, one in which the gay life is untethered to either hopeful futurity or resistance.

Bubbles grew up in SE Texas in the late 1970s and left for Austin soon after the AIDS crisis peaked in Texas in the mid-1980s. When I asked him if finding other gay people was difficult, he answered:

> You can ask any gay guy from Southeast Texas—and I mean, we all went to San Francisco and New York and Houston and Chicago and everything, so I mean—you ask any gay guy from down there, and they'll tell you. The best cruising was in Southeast Texas. The best—anywhere. You could go down to that park and there would be guys in the bushes, always, guys in the bathrooms. 'Cuz everybody was in the closet! But things changed there, everybody got sick. That's why I don't go back. Too many ghosts in Beaumont.

In Bubbles's telling, the utility of the closet does not necessarily function as a space for the avowal of the homosexual subject. On the contrary, the closet affords its inhabitants an opportunity for interactions understood not as shamefully covert, but as profoundly erotically charged zones of contact. Here, the public to whom or for whom you might emerge from the closet is not a collaborative force in the procedural events of "becoming" gay. In Bubbles's 1980s SE Texas, the straight public was a foil against which pleasure could be located in some augmented state, as the charge lied in finding pleasure despite the lack of a tolerant or progressive public to whom you might appeal. It was the already-charged atmosphere of the cruising spot, a by now familiar scene, made more intense by the perceived animosity of the world in which its sexual transactions took place and by its loss—a place now haunted by its revelers.

In the normative schema of progressive LGBTQ+ politics, these closeted actors might be considered the unfortunate victims of Deep South intolerance, conducting their transactions in the shame of secrecy and at the expense of their health. A traditional queer studies rebuke repurposes such characterizations, casting the scene of the cruise as the site of a communal, sexual transgression. In this way, interpretations of LGBTQ+ scenes of life are claimed by opposing ideological schemata: they are either gay or queer, either organized communities or dispersed publics, either assimilationist or resistant. This binary axis flattens the messiness of human lives into functional data for the purpose of furthering what remains a contestation over identity politics.

In SE Texas, self-described "gay rednecks" enacted zones of contact between gay/queer, Left/Right, and rural/urban binaries that trouble the oppositional qualities of each. As Tom Boellstorff asks in his call for a more capacious critique of same-sex marriage, "In what ways can our acts from within a system of power do more than sustain or not sustain that system?"[3] In this vein, I ask what a challenge to normative regimes might look like, not merely as a rational system or an intention, such as a revolution, but as internal destabilization. While important interventions have been made toward locating queer activism in rural spaces, this chapter is an attempt at locating a radical social ecology despite a marked lack of radical leftist activism.[4] What happens when the queer does not come home to roost in the country, as it were, but is found to have been there all along, in the ordinary lives and ordinary bodies of even its persecutors?

Bubbles performed drag in the 1980s in Beaumont. This was 1987, and SE Texas was being ravaged by the AIDS crisis. God was in the air—He came out of the refineries in a thick green miasmic fog. Bubbles's Mazda Miata ran out of gas one night in Vidor. He was in full drag, street pageantry: beaded fringed leather jacket, Annie Potts wig, and tight leopard dress. He was trying to flag somebody down off the feeder road of I-10. His Miata dead on the shoulder, red pumps in his hand. He was holding his thumb out and walking backward. He was in danger, and yet he conveyed a danger in his step, the heaviness of the scene's potentials warded off by the toughness of his gait. Two rednecks came up, thinking him a lady, and helped him, looking at his legs and leering the whole time. They pushed the Miata to a gas station; he walked in, careful not to speak to them or look them in the eyes. "I need gas," he said in a panicked stage whisper to the lady behind the counter, who looked at him, outside, and back at him, and intuitively understood his situation. He didn't describe her, but I can almost see her. The possibility of a character sprang up for me. An oversized sweatshirt and acid-blasted jeans, teased-up sprayed hair and feathered bangs, apathetically chewing gum or smoking a cigarette. A person always on the verge of rolling her eyes—the rhythm of her boring job elbowed in the ribs for a moment, a "what the hell was that" followed by a shrug. Bubbles filled the tank of his car, and the rednecks stood by. He made sure not to look to see the creeping confusion he knew would start to emerge on their faces. They were like his brothers, like his father, like his schoolmates.

The sun was going down, and the light changed. The harshness of lines in faces emerged under the yellow halide lamps of the gas station that gave off heat, scorching the june bugs that alighted upon them. The men got into their truck and followed Bubbles home. He turned onto his street, fists clenching the wheel—just knowing they would follow. But they kept on driving, giving him a lazy wave and a honk. They had merely continued the performance of character, accompanying the lady home. Bubbles was sure they had known. He said: "I think they just kept the game up"—they chose to follow through with the gallantry, and drove off entranced within the thrall of this encounter.

Decades later and hundreds of miles away, when we met by chance at the car dealership where he was working as a salesman, Bubbles told me this story. He told me he didn't like to go back to Beaumont anymore, that there were "too many ghosts there." His eyes filled with tears; he removed a hankie from his suit jacket pocket and dabbed at his eyes. He looked around at the other salesman and composed himself. "I'm not out here," he said. "I have to be careful. I'm not Bubbles here." The unexpected, surprising quality of this scene speaks to the register of different engagements with and around normativity with regard to expectation. What we have come to expect as a homophobic ordinary is unsettled. This unsettling is a thread that reaches to the foundations of the character of queerness in SE Texas, a character that is often constituted in terms of necessity and access—what is needed to make a queer character take place and what is known of models upon which to build them.

The queer scenes of SE Texas not only challenged queerness as emerging from an ideological viewpoint; they complicated queerness as an identity that sticks. It was not merely that queerness was not always attached to liberalism, but that its characters had different styles. Region was important, and the ways that region coalesced around ideas. It was not simply that LGBTQ+ folks in SE Texas lived in a region that lacked a leftist history of liberation, but that other important elements of the region infected any idea of queerness. The sociality this regionalism created was a context in which "normative" interaction existed in a different register, a different ordinary. Marisol de la Cadena's *not only*, an idea at least partially inspired by Strathernian relationality, resonates here, when she describes concepts as "not simply different; rather, differences existed (or came into being) along with similarities, which were never only that—but neither were differences. Controlling equivocations undermines analytical grammars that produce *either* (similar)-*or* (different) situations; and the undermining may be as constant as the either-or grammar is."[5]

In the stuck ecology of the SE Texan stories, the objective is not to characterize life in SE Texas as rigidly bound within unilateral forms of knowing and being. The resonances of SE Texas within broader US personhood are vital for conceiving of the possibility of life in a place characterized by both outsiders and inhabitants as beyond the pale, unthinkable. As de la Cadena notes, this requires the recognition of two key paradoxes: that similarities may occur differently, and differences may occur similarly. Queer people in SE Texas didn't always embody a character of queerness that ran *contra-* to the prevailing milieu of their surrounds. Queer rejection could come to signify under vastly different contexts; it depended what there was to reject, and what use rejection might or might not have.

Butch's Stories

Butch spent some of his early childhood in the mid-1950s in Sanford, Mississippi. His father was an itinerant laborer, and the family moved around a lot before settling in the Golden Triangle of SE Texas when the oil boom was still creating jobs and security for folks. His only friend in Sanford was Larry Schalls, the preacher's son. Larry's family owned the sawmill in town, and way back on their property was a huge mound of sawdust the boys used to play on. Butch spoke with a polite, clipped Texan twang, and tended to laugh quietly after each sentence. He told me about his formative days, and the moment that he experienced the discovery of queerness, the epiphany of recognition, and sometimes horror, that has been mythologized in LGBTQ+ literature and memoir. The queer epiphany is a hard-luck story subgenre.

> Walking down the street one evening, this older feller asked Larry if he would let him . . . suck his dick, his peepee. Larry didn't let him, I don't think, not that day anyway. So, I told my mom, and my mother said that some people have glandular problems. This is back in 1955–56. And so that was my experience of knowing about those things then. Wasn't long after that I was climbing a sweetgum tree in the yard, and something popped. I had climaxed. With my legs around that tree. Tried to climb the tree again, didn't work that time. It was just a few weeks later my mother told my father he needed to talk to me. You could hear everything in the house. I guess I was acting wiser. Well, he picked that very sweetgum tree to sit under—wanted to talk to me about the birds and the bees. And I was there just laughing to myself, because I already knew everything. [*laughs*] That was an intelligent but average person's opinion of something like that, back then. Never talked to Daddy about the glandular thing.

Thinking about the queer epiphany as hard-luck origin narrative, in both ethnographic and literary work, makes a connection between the stories queer people tell about their own self-discovery and the vast body of literature, from fiction to memoir to film, that shapes those tellings into a recognizable form. It also allows what I call a character of queerness who sits, sometimes uncomfortably, in the space between different traditions of queerness's function as a sociality and a politics.

Butch's origin narrative certainly describes an epiphany: the flash of realization, a beginning, and the generativity of a yet-to-come. Yet this anticipation differs from a hopeful futurity that remains anticipatory in the Muñozian sense. There is a definite arrival, almost banal in its instantiation, of queerness. There are the details of its development into a career, the tiresome daily tasks of dealing with others, and eventually, the ultimate disappointment and loss it brings. And in some sense, as Butch and other LGBTQ+ elders in the SE Texas region related to me, there is a definite feeling of its passage into the obsolete, the accrual of ordinary life around it that throws it together with disappointment. After Butch told me about his childhood and the way he kept this beginning to himself, away from his family, I asked him how he managed to have such a lucrative career in the insular gay scene of Beaumont without ever broaching the subject with his father—the family lived not even a half-mile away from the Copa, Butch's gay club, in Old Town.

Well, of course, much later there was a moment. It was the early '80s then, I guess, and I'm out on the patio talking to Daddy about nothing probably, and all of a sudden the words come out of his mouth: "Ain't it about time for you to go to work? Well, I'll take you." So I got ready, and off to the Copa we went. And he knew right where we were going. And that's the way the association of me and the Copa and Dad happened. But I don't know if he ever questioned anything or thought about it.

The silence of the double life, the willful ignorance and obfuscation of queerness's fact—these are the functional and banal impasses of the family and the practical matters of avoidance. Better to keep silent about it. It is another node along the way in the queer hard-luck origin narrative— the moment of turning from the family, into the world, sometimes onto the street or into the bar, to find other, potential, queer selves.

Butch is walking down Orleans Street in downtown Beaumont. Summer 1973. The midday Texan heat is forbidding. There is no escape from the sun. He's looking for he doesn't know what.

He described the feeling as somehow trying to orient to a zone of familiarity. "I was kinda searchin'—but I didn't know I was searchin.'"

After the moment of recognition, there comes the time of searching for others. This is the third stage of the queer epiphany story: the technique by which the queer person searches for a tether to the real of the queer world. Proof that this phenomenon, which might have until then only flickered as a desire, has some external grounding. This is what wandering does. Brings us into these zones of contact we didn't know we were searching for, honing in on a beacon, a signal. This is the way queer epiphany stories develop— the double realization of what is inside and what is outside, walking into the scene of the outside and feeling at home. Even if the feeling of home is unsettled, it is the feeling of having finally come to some proper alignment. James Baldwin describes it as a form of horror in his novel *Giovanni's Room*, in which the narrator comes to his epiphany through an unsettling encounter with a flaming queer whom he has rebuffed in a Paris bar. The man points to him and tells him that he will burn in a fire. This statement is taken to mean that his queer desire will emerge and consume him: the character will make himself known, regardless of his intentions. Far away from the vibrancy of a queer Paris scene, Butch described the same sort of moment as finding a lifeline and stumbling haphazardly upon kismet.

Butch passed a bar called the Farmhouse: "These were the days in Beaumont when the idea of a gay bar—well, there was no idea of a gay bar."

The original Farmhouse was in Houston, off of Westheimer in the heart of gay town. The owners opened another one in Beaumont; under what inspiration, Butch could only speculate. In his version of the story, the gay couple who owned the Farmhouse were splitting up, so one of them came out to Beaumont and bought the bar. They changed the name to the Copa in 1979.

The bar is dark, there are a few people sitting along its cool edge in the shadows, but he can't make out their faces. He senses something different. He gets scared, walks on. Hears a woman's voice call out, bawdy and raspy, cutting across the air in the violent heat. "Wanna blowjob?" followed by the raucous laughter of some infernal gang, the sound of which makes him shiver. He composes himself, stops. Turns around and walks back in.

"And that was Fat Mary. She hung out with the gay crowd and was such a character. She'd always be yelling out stuff like that. Died some years back. That was before I knew anything."

This first voice arrests him—the first encounter with character. Fat Mary knows something about him that he is only beginning to work out. This is significant. He walks back in and gets a beer. The small crowd is jovial, but distant somehow, the Texan way. He tries to use the bathroom but finds it occupied by bodies writhing about, entwined on the floor. Gets nervous, walks out again.

"And I kept going back, and sort of became familiar with them. And then of course years later I bought it, after working there for two years. The owners had gone on vacation and asked me to take care of the bar. I guess I had a reputation in Beaumont. A secure one, a good one."

At the time of my research, Butch still owned the Copa, SE Texas's most infamous gay bar. In his midseventies, he suffered from macular degeneration and was almost completely blind. He sat alone in his house in the cool of his dark living room, just down the street from downtown Beaumont and the shuttered nightclub. He told me about gay life in this region, stories of struggle and hard luck built up with a tragicomic feeling. They carried the weight of some grand narration—as though he was regaling me with myth; his tone was nearly surprised at the events it recounted. The objects he spoke of but could no longer see lay in piles around him—he hoarded the memorabilia of the Copa in great chests and file cabinets filled with drag queen headshots and flyers advertising events. Divine performed there in 1983. "I bet she couldn't believe she was booked in this crummy town." Butch chuckled. "On her way to Houston or somewhere better, I would think." He was voicing the classic attitude of cosmopolitan gay culture: that gay life thrives in cities and passes over rurality with disdain. But his own attitude was clearly ambivalent, as he had stayed in Beaumont for his whole life, eking out a living as one of the city's most visible and active gay advocates from the 1970s to the 1990s. He told me he was close to being a millionaire at one time. But the money all went. What it was lost on was a dark memory, something better left unsaid. Like the great oil barons who found their fortune at Spindletop and sapped the land of its riches, just a few miles down the road, there was the feeling of the queer epiphany leading Butch to a grand discovery, one that he harnessed and saw to its conclusion.

The story of the Copa is exemplary of the messy, unexpected quality of queerness in the region. After the owners took over the Farmhouse in the late 1970s and revamped it, the Copa was unsurprisingly an object of local scorn, targeted by vandalism and anger. "People used to run from their cars into the Copa, with their jackets covering their faces. It was a different time. You couldn't be gay." What is surprising, however, is that the Copa quickly became downtown Beaumont's greatest moneymaker and soon had the protection and begrudging respect of the Beaumont police force and officials. Beaumont's regional planner was evidently a gay man, who Butch said could often be found "drunk underneath our pool table." The regional planner's influence made the shift from taboo nightclub to local boon more seamless.

There is a story of queer redemption in the region, under the banner of something like white respectability politics. For example, more than one person in SE Texas told me about a gay dentist out in Baytown during the 1960s and 1970s who was well loved in the community because, as Butch said, he "kept to himself, dressed real nice, and always had a smile on his face." The regional way of not looking too deeply into things, a Texan civility, colored the stories with a sense of politeness, as well as an underlying dread of being found out.

This precarity, which fluctuates between global and regional ideas of what queerness is and what it can do, draws from Martin Manalansan's interest in looking at "queerness as productively constituted by mess and disorder."[6] In the context of queer types revealed by ethnographic research in SE Texas, the precise value of this mess not only sheds light on queer regionalism and new developments in rural queer studies, but also acts as a signpost for how queerness travels as a type of character.[7] This revelation does not merely deny the lingua franca of academic cosmopolitan queerness in rural areas. Instead, it uses description to present a different model of queerness, which takes as its departure point not a cleaving away of radicalism, but an inner erosion of normative types. This model is present in local queer understandings of self, and the enmeshment of the queer self in the regional scene. It is not necessarily that queerness creates a different subjectivity in SE Texas, but that the qualities of the region and the attribution of what queerness is capable of enacting ask us to face the "queer mess" of difference in a deeper sense.

Butch's Eye Appointment

I picked Butch up at his house in Beaumont to bring him to his eye appointment. He was sitting crouched on the front steps in a torn T-shirt and baggy cargo pants. He lived in Old Town, next to the abandoned home he grew up in—"Grandma's house"—an early twentieth-century American Foursquare home with a decaying wraparound porch and massive live oaks covering it mostly from street view. No one lived there anymore. Its last inhabitant was Butch's brother—a convicted murderer-rapist who killed a Black man over a game of pool in 1973, slitting his throat and dragging him into a ditch. The brother had a stroke and was living in a nursing home up in the country. So the house abided, empty in its decaying splendor.

Butch got into my car, handing me a paper doggie bag from some long-closed restaurant and saying, "Happy Birthday." It was my birthday, and I had forgotten that until earlier that morning. Inside the bag was a sprig of rosemary from his garden and a candle from his house. I thanked him, and he waved my thanks away imperiously: "Oh, it's nothing." He didn't look at me. Butch had a kind of involuntary humming refrain, a descending staccato melody—"bmp . . . bmp . . . bmp"—whenever there was a pause in the conversation. It was quiet, barely noticeable at first, but I noticed that it became louder and more persistent in stressful situations.

We drove over to the Eye Center. On the way, he told me that he had started an initiative in Beaumont in the 1970s to have a recycling center built—he pointed it out as we passed it. He said practically no one recycles in this area, because it costs extra to have a truck come to your home. You have to trek downtown to the center where hobos will harass you as you try to sort your papers from your plastics, or so the stories went. Most people burned their trash in a large oil barrel in their backyard. People had burn piles as a matter of course. The air filled with smoke, or the smell of burning. It blended in with the other clouds of airborne stuff.

Butch was probably telling the truth about having something to do with the center's planning and construction, but the extent of his truth has always left me wondering. The actual story might recast him as a peripheral player who gave the initiative some money, or he could really have been at the helm. There is almost no way of knowing. I many times went to the historical library in Beaumont after he told me a strange story about some bureaucratic goings on in town, only to reach some dead end in the microfiche. And when I asked him to tell me again, he'd change or shift some key element of the story so that I doubted what I had heard. He didn't lie so much as adorn his stories with expressive flourishes that left the matter of truth somehow obsolete.

When we arrived at the Eye Center, it hadn't yet opened for business, and I wondered whether he had gotten the time wrong. It was 7:30. He banged at the sliding glass doors, peering in and probably not seeing the emptiness. A side entrance was open, so we entered, but the space was hardly lit and quite empty. "We'll wait here," he said. We stood in the corridor for a few minutes, until a young woman entered from the side door holding a coffee. She was in pink scrubs, clearly a receptionist or tech. She paused when she saw us and then proceeded to pass us, giving us a very intense stare. Butch greeted her in his dandyish way, and she grunted and told us we could sit in the waiting room. "Y'all can go sit in there—that's where people wait." She wore a Jesus fish pin on her lapel. She couldn't have been more than twenty-three, but her demeanor suggested an older, matronly woman, a person well practiced in the art of being that type of character. There is a professionalization that encourages this presentation of self. We went and sat in the waiting room. Butch got up very close to the television to look for the power button. He couldn't see it. I went over and turned it on, and we sat down. He was nervous. He shuffled and swung his feet—the intensity of his humming reached a peak.

A few minutes later, an overly friendly nurse approached us. These were the two modes of sociality we encountered that day—either brusque circumspection or civil Texan etiquette. She spoke to Butch in a bright drawl that bounced mercilessly against the drab ecru art of the waiting room and its fluorescent-lit glare: "Good morning, Mr. Keller! We're almost ready for you! In the future, maybe don't come in through the side door. You kinda scared someone." And she was gone, smiling widely as she fled and I scrambled to find some retort. Butch appeared unruffled; he always maintained the appearance of the smug humming aristocrat, although I could see by the frozen nature of his smirk that he was slightly embarrassed. I realized that there was a performance of class taking place in all of Butch's interactions with the outside world, a performance that could no longer be substantiated by his class status but remained as a vestigial display. The young woman who had first come in passed again in the corridor. Surely this was who we had scared. "Scared you, huh?" Butch said and snickered. She did not pause but kept walking, head held high and proud. "Not scared, you just kinda startled me," she said. "You startled me too," Butch said, but she either didn't hear or chose not register us any longer. She passed. The way he said that was unmistakably catty—it was gay in a recognizable "art of the insult" way. Something about the humor in the phrase suggested that she had startled him not because of her sudden appearance, but because of her physical appearance in general. I wondered how I knew to read into the phrase that deeply.

Butch abruptly wanted to show me the Eye Center—he became animated in his anxiety—he wanted to give me a tour. We walked around the waiting room and the adjacent larger waiting room, which had begun to fill with people, mostly elderly, many of whom seemed to be watching gospel music videos on their phones, creating a dissonant aural field. They looked up at us with suspicion or apathy. I was beginning to feel like a suspicious person, in fact. The friendly nurse called Butch again, this time to the counter to sign paperwork. He ignored her beckoning, pointing out this and that element of the interior, the fake plants, the anachronistic art that combined some Arabic and ancient Greek motifs, the carpeting that had molded. "Butch, I think they're calling you." "Oh, *are* they?" he said quite loudly. He was resisting. This was all part of the process for him. He had been doing this for seven decades. We approached the counter, and the young receptionist (a different one than the first, startled one), seemingly embarrassed by us, had him sign some paperwork. "What is *this* and what is *that*?" he wanted to know, suddenly all business. "Oh, this is just a release form saying you are getting shots in your eyeballs, and we won't be responsible for you getting home afterwards, so if you stumble and fall then we don't have to help pick you up." Or something like that. He hummed and signed. She asked him for his co-pay. He was affronted, made a big scene. "I've never had to pay before!" It was $40. She said this time was different for some insurance reason that was too boring for him to hear. I paid the co-pay, hoping that my balance wasn't in the negative. It went through, to my relief. He was affronted anew. "How dare they—we'll get to the bottom of this!" he said to me conspiratorially. He hummed. They called him into the back. "Mr. Keller! We're ready for you!"

He wanted me to see them do it, he said. Although later he claimed that he had asked me and I had agreed heartily, I was actually a bit squeamish but thought it'd be good to witness. And I wanted to protect him from any further dehumanizing elements. We were led to the examination room, which had a medieval setup—elaborate structures meant to hold the head in place, hold the eyes open, position the body for an optic exam. He sat exuding calm and panic simultaneously, humming. A new nurse came in with her hair up in a tight bun, deigning to smile at us. Sitting in the corner, I was positioned in front of her at the desk on the computer, with Butch just behind, spotlit in the chair. She asked him routine diagnostic questions. He said his eyes were fine, but "TV tired" (fatigued from watching too much television) because he never slept anymore. She asked if he was on any new medications since last time. He was evasive; he asked her if she was on any new medications since last time. She said no. Her happy face was beginning to show signs of crumbling. The mascara twitched. She couldn't properly bring off the maternal performance of the nurse with Butch, who stymied the conversation for my benefit or some unseen audience of Truman Capotes. It wasn't clear whom he was playing to.

She began administering the exam, during which he elegantly held a device to his eyes like a lorgnette and attempted to identify lines of letters on a screen that was actually behind him—he was looking at it through a mirror in front of him, which was directly behind me. He started: "F . . . um . . . F . . . bmp bmp bmp . . . um. . . . This is how I drive, Joey . . . um, F . . ." He couldn't go further; he was laughing quietly. She wasn't much amused. I wanted to warn him not to mention his blind driving. She made some notes on the computer. I think I saw her shake her head, but it was dark. The lights came back up, and she prepared to leave. He told her he looked forward to the drops in his eyes that acted as an anesthetic before the injections because they created bright, kaleidoscopic visions behind his eyelids. He called them "psychedelic." She winced politely. "The doctor will be in to see you shortly." And she was gone.

The doctor entered almost immediately, a large, well-groomed man with impeccable fingernails. He was fresh from golf or Houston. He wasn't happy, but wasn't angry. He had an inscrutable air. "Hello, Mr. Keller," he said, barely concealing the irritation. The nurses had warned him, I thought. He moved with a grace unlikely for such a body. He noticed me peripherally. The over-friendly nurse who had asked Butch not to come in the side entrance reappeared suddenly from a hidden door. "Comin' up behind ya, Mr. Keller!" she said, with a stinging cheerfulness. She had arrived to help administer the injection; there would only be one today, it turned out, in the right eye. The doctor placed a spring into Butch's right eye socket, placating him ("I know this is the hard part") as it lodged between his socket and upper eyelid and held the eyeball open like the torture scene in *A Clockwork Orange*. Butch's knuckles gripped the armrests, as they tilted him backward in his chair. The doctor raised the syringe, which Butch had described as having an audible quality as the needle pierced the skin of the retina, and the injection was administered. The doctor said something at that time, and Butch afterward told me that the doctor's utterance had caused him to turn his eyeball toward the doctor, which scarred the eyeball and left a bruise. "Doctor, this is my friend Joey Russo. He's doing a PhD," Butch said. I realized that I represented a form of cultural capital for him in the context of professionals. The doctor feigned interest, saying something sidelong to me like "Well, that sounds busy," before asking Butch about his eye health. Butch remained evasive. The doctor explained the kaleido-scopic imagery, which had something to do with light and angles, and left us hurriedly, wishing me luck.

On the car ride home, I asked Butch if he had known an older gay man about whom I had been told a story. It seemed that the man was wealthy, and lived on Long Street in Beaumont. Some arsonists had burned down his home and scrawled "faggot" all over his erotic portraits. He was in his home at the time, and had to climb out onto his balcony with his dog in order to be saved by the fire department. He had to leave Beaumont after that. Butch didn't know him, but said that a lot of "bad gay stuff" happened on Long Street. In 1985, a cowboy friend of his put a shotgun to his mouth and pulled the trigger because he couldn't handle being gay. "He couldn't keep his hands off of me," Butch chuckled as he climbed out of my car. Later, he clarified that the suicide had taken place on Louisiana Street, not Long Street, and that he had confused the two streets because they were adjacent. He said that the cowboy was a "real cowboy," not a "gay cowboy," implying that he was not able to reconcile his masculine image with his desire, that the aesthetics of both could not coalesce.

I watched Butch walk up the porch steps and into his house. As the months passed, we stopped seeing much of each other. The last I heard, he had sold the Copa, and there was a period without running water in his house for reasons that were never made clear to me. He called me a few years after I left the area and started in as though we'd just seen each other the day before. He told me with some pride that the drunk regional com-missioner who had napped under the Copa's pool table was still alive and living in Houston, and that I ought to get in touch with him—*he* had the largest collection of gay books in the great state of Texas.

Four.

Ringing Out

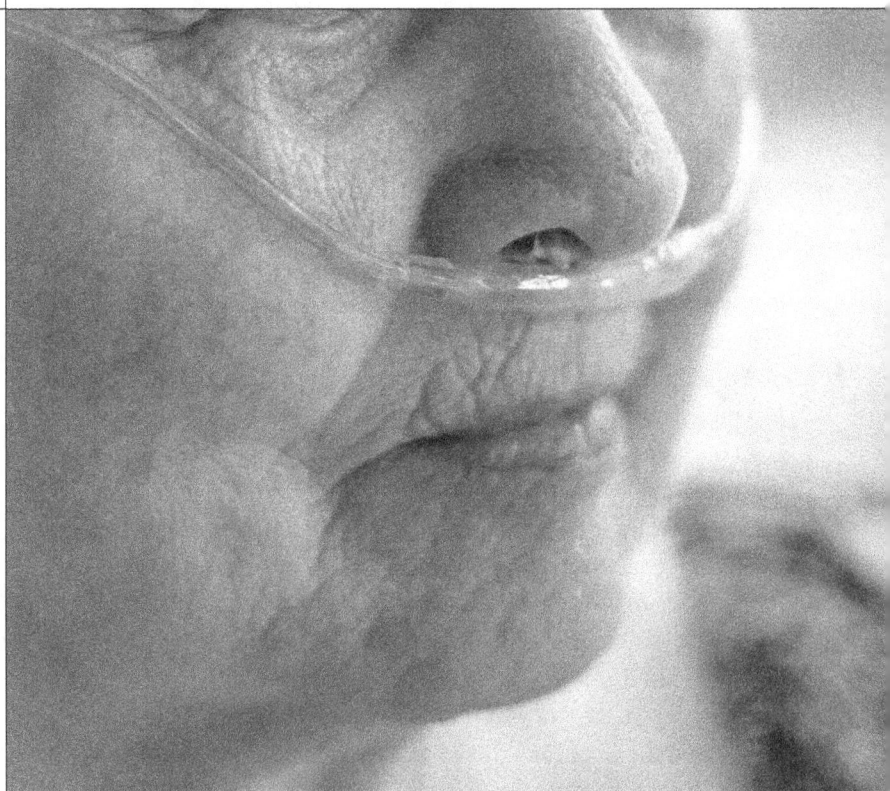

The Flatlands

Every morning at 4:45, Lurleen fired up the griddle at the Valero station and waited for her "fellers." They would start to trickle in around 5:30, old-timers trudging along the country highway on foot, some rolling up in old rusty Chevy pickups with fat hoods. They came from the farm-to-market roads, and a few from right there in town. They had been meeting for breakfast and morning stories every day for about three decades—before the Valero station, there was another gas station, and before that, a feed store. Lurleen (or Lulu, as some of the fellers call her) had been behind the griddle there for as long as any of them could remember, and she was never late with their coffee and sausage sandwiches or kolaches. "Only difference is now it's real clean in there and she can't smoke," said the landlord. The fellers enjoyed the Valero, because it had large windows and tables in the front, and they could "set awhile" and enjoy the morning sun as it saturated every crease in their leathery faces that have spent a lifetime facing the Texas sun in fields with no shade. A few of their sons worked at the Valero or Motiva refineries down in Port Arthur, and they told stories of power changing hands there, of entire staff laid off in moments of callous desperation, of workers sick from fumes whose lawsuits never bore fruit. And yet they came every day to sit in the cool space of the Valero station for a bit of respite before the workday began, off to their menial jobs in town or to sit somewhere else for the rest of the day.

Unless there was some pressing matter that merited immediate consideration, such as a car broken down on the highway, the driver drunk or high and raving at 6 a.m.—or maybe one of them missed a car note payment and feared the consequences—the story event began in an unspoken ritualized fashion. One would give the prompt: "Now Larry, you know Larry out my way." One would laugh, shaking his head. In this way, the story was evoked and given its mood—one of circumspect and suspicious caution or perplexity at the bedevilment of this old town that used to be "real nice." But then there were meth heads at the Redbud Festival and no jobs. A dog might wander right into the yard from God knows where, and you'd just have to shoot him because the owners "don't pay him no mind"—nods of agreement from the rest. And the long beat of silence, all looking out the large windows at the pumps, hands rested on canes, and the occasional hacking cough. Eventually, one of them would slowly rise with a drawn out "Well . . . I'll see you boys later," and the air would change. They came back to themselves. They would raise a hand in farewell to Lurleen in the back at the griddle underneath the "Kountry Kitchen" sign and head out to meet whatever the day brought, same as yesterday—same as tomorrow.

The land in SE Texas is so flat that the experience of traversing it seems suspended, illusory. It is not only that the land is flat, but that the images repeat in a way not seen in other places with the same uniformity. It has the effect of an old movie where the characters are in a car that passes the same background again and again. Power lines, cattle in pasture, dollar store, church, power lines, cattle in pasture, dollar store. You pass stand after stand of pine, a field, expansive and wide, then a set of shacks or trailers. Then the whole thing repeats almost identically. This is seen, but it is also felt as a closing and opening: the closeness of the pines or the town suddenly absent; the suffocating, sealed space opened to the expanse of the cattle pasture where the horizon comes straight down to the ground itself in many places on account of the lack of buildings. The sky is perpetually dotted with black and turkey vultures, aloft on thermal drafts and practically motionless in the air, hovering. Or when the day is cloudy, they are perched on the power lines or amassed atop the latticed steel transmission towers, or hopping and hissing along the road's shoulder, pulling the entrails from a dog or possum carcass.

Entering town, all of the images of a banal small-town Texas scene emerge. Everything slows down as the speed trap begins. The sudden panoply of fast-food signs reaching high into the air, the feed store followed by the Dollar General, followed by two or four gas stations on competing corners in the main intersection. The church, displaying its plastic banners with reinforced eyelets, against abortion. The abandoned buildings, covered in kudzu. Pickup trucks dominate the road, a fleet of white Ford F-150s, F-350s, "duallys." There is an obsession with tinted windows. Certain decals insinuate things about drivers—Calvin (of the Calvin & Hobbes comic) peeing means there is a badass guy in there; a pink barbed-wire border means a feminine but tough lady, a set of testicles hung from a tow hitch means something about masculinity, depending on who you ask. Could be just funny or could be overcompensation.

RealTree and other forest-pattern camouflage is the unspoken uniform here. A pattern originally designed for hunting and outdoorsmen that really took off in the 1980s with Mossy Oak, RealTree now commonly dominates leisure garb, the upholstery of vehicles, and even formalwear. It has become an ingrained Texan aesthetic, signifying a broad swath of qualities, an aestheticization of rurality itself. As a trend, it is the mass production of an aesthetic that, like many subcultural trends, originally signified an almost iconoclastic sensibility. In this case, camo might signify a slow, even willfully or rebelliously, backward and anti-urban way of life, like a reflexive visual code that knows what it is doing. It becomes a mutual recognition point. People see "redneck" in it, they see "poor whites," or they see Trump and bad feelings and clinging to the Confederacy. But this stereotyping of character is complicated by the middle class's adoption of it to the point of frivolity, not to mention its presence among rural people across the nation, and rural people of color, such as in the small unincorporated town of Bon Wier, Texas, where I spoke with young Black men who were wearing it both while hunting and while just hanging out.

But forest camo is also the visual regimentation of natural patterns made synthetic and covering all manner of common goods, from lunchboxes to galoshes to wallets to slippers. It blankets common items with the veneer of the natural, and in wearing it, you participate in an "eco-pageantry," dressed as the forest itself. The original purpose of this pageantry—the need for the hunter to conceal itself from its prey—has become obsolete in the quotidian encompassing of it, in its explosion as a visual trend—beyond the fixation with a brand. It is like the rising popularity of a plaid, for instance, but more heavily loaded with regional associations.

In the towns, there are squat, beige municipal buildings with mysterious purposes, some windowless. They range from courthouse to pump shed, functional little pods dotting the landscape. There is almost always a main restaurant in town, a buffet eatery or country diner of some kind that is filled with senior citizens, but is being rendered obsolete by the fast-food chains whose signs reach far into the sky so as to be seen from afar. The signs display encrypted shorthand code to their customers, whose trucks line up around the buildings' drive-thrus at all hours. One Burger King had a sign that I puzzled over for some time before deciphering its message: "Tues Bogo HB 5–8." Deb, the landlord's wife, translated for me: "Tuesday, Buy One, Get One Hamburgers, 5 p.m. to 8 p.m." A person's week might be scheduled around that BOGO Tuesday in the absence of affordable quality foods.

Out on one of these endless, flat rural highways in Jasper County sat the Poor Man Shop—an unlikely dot interrupting the vista. It was unclear whether the sign in front, "Poor Man Shop," was describing or identifying the place of business. The Poor Man Shop sold Nomex suits for refinery workers.[1] Its front yard filled with junk, the Poor Man Shop displayed the dystopian late-industrial scene of SE Texas, what Fortun describes as "a historical period characterized by degraded infrastructure, exhausted paradigms, and the incessant chatter of new media."[2] It sat under the shadow of the refineries, blasting flames from their flares, shadowing the land in darkness. The proprietor of the Poor Man's Shop was an old-timer with a beard who could always be found among the junk, fixing a broken appliance or standing and looking at his hoarded collection. He listened to the radio and hummed to himself. On some days, he was very talkative and friendly. But mostly, he would give you a sidelong glance and return to what he was doing. There was a time that another sign by the roadside welcomed passersby. On one visit, I noticed most of his stuff had been moved to another location up the road, and a large sign at the new location said, "No Stopping."

Refinery workers would rise in the morning or the evening, depending on their shift, and approach the monoliths rising from the flat land. They drove through the smoke. The workers' lungs and hands and skin were covered in the smoke's detritus, and everyone's kin would breathe the presence of it when they brought it home. They bought Nomex suits and wore masks and gloves and good boots to protect themselves from the burns and spills. Their skin had to be covered, and steps had to be followed. Proficiency in using eyewashes had to be taught. Contact numbers for emergency services and disaster controls had to be clearly posted. In Evadale (called "evil smell" by Deb), off Highway 96, the stench of the nearby paper mill pervaded the air at all hours. It caused headaches and burning nostrils. A little roadside trailer café called the Lunch Box never served any customers, at least that I saw. The region was locked into this relationship with contingency, the inevitability of debilitation, and the story of pressing on despite that, because there wasn't anything else to do. It was covered in a film of cancer, under which life was happening and through which it was transforming. The bodies under the film knew it and felt it in the air, even felt that they were becoming transformed into whatever "it" was.[3]

Cancer and the Ringing-Out Form

After her final radiation treatment, Deb walked back into the waiting room with her oxygen tank in tow. She rang a bell on the wall, mounted on a plaque with an inscription that read: "Ringing Out—Ring this bell, three times well, its toll to clearly say, my treatments done, this course is run, and now I'm on my way." The waiting room broke out in applause; a woman yelled, "Amen!" Deb turned to me and said, "Get me out of here." She was having trouble keeping a smile on her face, her exhaustion creeping through. Deb had been battling inoperable squamous cell lung carcinoma for almost a year. She'd had thirty-five courses of radiation treatment and had been alternating radiation and chemotherapy treatments downstairs in the chemo clinic.

The stuck relation to place is deepened in attunements to somatic function, which extend feeling things in the air, beyond attention paid to ideological attachments.[4] Bodies can also feel things in the air, quite literally, and these attunements magnify the stark disconnect between interior and exterior that mark the region as an encapsulated space. What Nicholas Shapiro calls "bodily knowledge" structures a poetics of storytelling forms in SE Texas that I heard as a ringing out—a resonant form that describes what a region can do to a body, and that body's transmission of these effects into the cancer sufferer's accounts of what happened to them.[5] To ring out is to throw one's story into the cacophony of histories of suffering, the power of the petrochemical industry, medical knowledge, the practice of suspicion, and the eventual submission to sickness's inevitability. Rob Nixon characterizes the effects that I see as leading to the ringing-out storytelling form as the "slow violence" of ignored and aggravated environmental crises on the poor.[6] For my informants and friends in the cancer center, the storytelling form was a way of speaking both back to and from within the effects of the slow violence of the petrochemical industry and, therefore, late industrialism.

The resonant form of cancer stories connects these elements, and SE Texans deployed the stories actively to form a suspicious category—a troubled commons of sufferers that dwells in the ambivalent space between seeking care and "knowing better, "invoking an attachment that sees what is "really happening" to bodies under the shadow of the refineries.[7] The commons produced by cancer is an exhausted one; the ringing out of SE Texan cancer stories were an affective response to "a distinct unwillingness in both the scientific and business communities to address environmental causes of cancer."[8]

When Deb was first diagnosed with squamous cell lung carcinoma, her oncologist staged the cancer and gave her a hopeful prognosis of treatment despite the impossibility of surgery. This was due to the proximity of the tumor to her aorta. Deb was a lifelong heavy smoker who, like a surprising number of cancer patients, claimed to have developed cancer very soon after quitting and attributed a causal relationship to cessation and the emergence of cancer in the body. Deb's oncologist dismissed this phenomenon as incidental; he suggested that it is a common occurrence because smokers often quit at a point when their body has been pushed to its limit and symptoms associated with respiratory illness become more pronounced. However, the idea that there could be some correlation between abrupt smoking cessation and the development of lung cancer persisted among some of the lung cancer patients I spoke with, despite scarce evidence to support this claim. This suspicion, along with a number of other beliefs and superstitions, structured a mode of dealing with illness that positioned the sufferer as a healthy skeptic whose trust should never be fully placed in the for-profit medical-industrial complex.

Skepticism was a recurrent theme throughout my time at the cancer ward in Beaumont. It created a tension between reasonable and unreasonable expectations and beliefs about what the health-care industry could provide, what the health-care industry revealed as a set of knowledge about treatment and the body, and, most importantly, what it withheld or misled about this knowledge. More than a few cancer patients I spoke with made connections between what they called "Big Oil" and "Big Pharma," shorthand terminology for the petrochemical and healthcare industries, respectively. A few of these folks, who were sometimes characterized by their peers as "conspiracy theorists" or "conspiracy people," even suggested that these industries were in cahoots with one another on some level, the implication being that there was a cyclical and, indeed, diabolical relationship between them that boiled down to profit. The petrochemical industry employed workers whose health was adversely affected by the conditions of labor, thereby supplying the local healthcare industry with patients, which in turn provided care that allowed the labor force to return to work. A woman in the elevator of the cancer ward said to me: "Now, what do you suppose they up to at the doctor's office when they give you this whole course of treatment? That isn't a coincidence—*I'm telling you*. All these people here, all these men—they're refinery men, they come down from the refineries and that made them sick. They come down here, and they get all this expensive treatment—well, they say it makes you better. And so they can work again. It's like that!" When I asked her why such a vast conspiracy wasn't common knowledge, she told me, "People have been asking that question for years, I'm telling you that." That was not the first time I had heard mention of "people" in this sense—a community of questioners and skeptics. An in-group—those "in the know." Yet what simultaneously existed in many of the stories about cancer and Big Oil was a community of people who were not questioning, who "didn't know better" than to continue to labor within and under the shadow of the refineries. There was a constant tension between those who knew and those who did not—and the examples culled from these publics overlapped. The conspicuous absence of environmental watchdog groups (although some existed—many times from other states and came occasionally to monitor activity in SE Texas) confirmed the strange state of limbo regarding attention paid to the ill effects of the petrochemical industry on the region, and whether that attention had any consequence.

Some of the cancer patients at the ward were suspicious of receiving medical treatment at the MD Anderson Cancer Center/Memorial Hermann Health System in Houston, just eighty-five miles to the west. MD Anderson consistently ranked in the top five cancer research and treatment centers in the United States, but the SE Texans I spoke to generally viewed it as either unreliable (despite its consistently highly ranked success numbers), too expensive (despite in-network insurance rates not differing for most SE Texans insurance policies), or too distant (despite being less than a hundred miles from Beaumont city center). When her family suggested the possibility of receiving superior treatment there, Deb rejected the idea. She'd had bad experiences in Houston, she said, as had members of her family who had died of cancer and cancer-related illness in the past. This was undoubtedly true. Both of Deb's parents died from forms of cancer related to asbestosis. Her father worked in construction and came home every day for decades in asbestos-seeped coveralls. Her mother would wash his work uniform in their gas dryer; she contracted respiratory cancer that was apparently attributed to her contact with the toxic materials. Whether this was the official cause was never made clear to me, and whether it was attributed by the doctors or by other, more mysterious diagnostics was also left open. Deb and her family did not subscribe to what they saw as conspiracy theories about Big Oil and Big Pharma, but they did question the complacency on the part of both the government and locals in excavating possible connections between the petrochemical industry and health in the region. Deb said to me on a number of occasions that she "wouldn't be surprised if something was going on."

Domestic secondhand exposure became a common story of the mid-twentieth century in SE Texas, although its consequences were not seen until the latter part of the century.[9] Its effects led to a surge in SE Texas in law firms representing cancer sufferers, and a proliferation of lawsuits against petrochemical and construction companies in the 1990s, with varying degrees of success. The spike in lawsuits, however, did little or nothing to change cancer-related mortality rates. During the latter part of her cancer treatment, after a tumor was discovered in her brain, Deb eventually began receiving treatments in Houston at Memorial Hermann, after she began to question the attentiveness of her oncologist in Beaumont.

A sacrifice zone is a place designated for destruction so that capital may grow. The entire Refinery Belt, from Corpus Christi, Texas, to Pascagoula, Mississippi, is a sacrifice zone for the petrochemical industry. This became especially evident after the BP Deepwater Horizon oil spill in 2010. The paradox of seeing the necropolitical within what is commonly understood to be a successful capitalist society requires recognizing gradations of the politics resulting in industrial and postindustrial death that do not bear the hallmark of the necropolitical image. This is the necropolitical couched in the pastoralism of the American South mythos, the picnic table spread under the magnolia tree and an honest day's work for everybody who wants it. I use Joyelle McSweeney's idea of the necropastoral, which incorporates modes such as seepage to describe an obscured process of toxic materials slowly being absorbed into the atmosphere, air, and water, as well as into bodies.[10]

Theories of biosociality make links between environmental stimuli and various personality disorders and mental illnesses, as well as uncovering broader connections between human biology and culture. Studies in biocultural anthropology have suggested that political economy is shaped by culture, determining resource availability, access to and attitudes toward disease protection, and beliefs surrounding health maintenance.[11] The petrochemical industry as a product of late-capitalist economic endeavor has had an ubiquitous effect upon the sacrifice zone of Texas's Refinery Belt; it has altered the baseline understanding of what health is (and what healthy looks like) in a region where air quality ranks among ProPublica's worst regions for cancer risk.[12] By centering production in small city centers surrounded by remote rural areas, it also has necessitated a lifestyle that requires consumers to travel long distances to perform labor as well as to access quality produce and healthcare. Lifestyle "choices," long considered one of the primary causes of cancer deaths, must be understood under the constraint of bad air, food deserts and near-deserts, and the on-the-fly life-style of working-class laborers. Attributing blame to either environmental or lifestyle factors becomes impossible, as the two form a stuck ecology in which choice is under considerable constraint. I suggest extending the definition of biosociality to include the forms of sociality produced by the adverse effects of industry upon bodies, such as the paradox of labor-ing despite the knowledge of danger, the cultivation of a mythos of hard luck around this condition, and the ease by which other health concerns can be dismissed, considering the pall of ill health that can cover a region like a shadow.

Cancer as a biosocial event joins and animates the lives of its suffer-ers through stories and the sharing of space. It thrives even in the face of looming death. It is an almost morbidly ideal scene for watching the ways in which America's death sensibility rings out in the lives and stories of those in its thrall. It is a place where the intractable trajectory of American capitalist venture comes home to roost in an ecology that is germinating all of the bad feelings and bad scenes: "the end of the world." But it is an end that we have already seen, a crisis that we continue to observe playing out before us. As James Berger noted just before the end of the twen-tieth century, "This sense of crisis has not disappeared, but in the late twentieth century it exists together with another sense, that the conclusive catastrophe has already occurred, the crisis is over . . . and the ceaseless activity of our time—the news with its procession of almost indistinguish-able disasters—is only a complex form of stasis."[13] SE Texas is a dystopian American scene not only in the sense that its major industry, Big Oil, is one of the most significant contributors to impending ecological collapse, but in that its populace are the phantoms often pointed to by media outlets as those *doing harm*, the ones whose ideological apparatus has become so embedded in the machinations of America as to keep these environmen-tally harmful processes in place. It is a place where people not only "vote against their best interests," but also *live* against them. The complexity of

the political situation emerges when their interests, the ones they supposedly so foolishly ignore, are revealed to be vastly different than what is expected. That is, the interests that they are assumed to be voting against are
etic—and in the rhetoric of voting against one's best interests, the accusa-
tion of backwardness is usually leveled at them from the sphere of modern
secular humanism. In the end, there is some level of projection occurring in
which the best interests of a society are taken to be universal. For many in
SE Texas, "best interests" are not necessarily a long-term self-preservation
of humanity that coalesces in a liberal conservationist model. Here, con-
servation is more attuned to an idea of active, dominant stewardship that
is more interested in wrangling, harnessing, and subduing nature than in
"harmonizing" with it.

It might be more accurate to say that these are different methods of
achieving a harmonic model under which the structure of environmentalism becomes complicated. Under the rubric of something like climate
change awareness, a huge segment of the population must be characterized as "deniers" in order to legitimize the highly substantiated points of
climate change research. They must be characterized as exhibiting some
macrosuicidal characteristic or intense pursuit of nihilism that actively
seeks the end of human life or the end of a human-inhabited Earth. There
are countless stories picked up by local media outlets about the SE Texan's
"anti-environmentalist" sensibilities, usually concerning an interaction
with local wildlife that flies in the face of sympathetic, or even logical,
ideas about what the relationship of humans to their environment should
look like.

McSweeney's description of the necropastoral, a mode "in which the
fact of mankind's depredations cannot be separated from an experience
of 'nature' which is poisoned, mutated, aberrant, spectacular, full of ill effects and affects," finds one of its nodes in the machinations of capital (the
churning out of bodies made sick and unfit for service in the refineries) in
SE Texas.[14] McSweeney outlines the processes of the necropastoral, chief
among them in this work being seepage—a process in which the SE Texan
is engaged so deeply that it has come to constitute ordinary life. Besides
deeply affecting the baseline idea of environmental and wildlife stewardship and death, the necropastoral in this instance is also the poetic element of Shapiro's chemosphere—it is the moment of the petrochemical
industry's seepage into bodies in the form of cancer stories, in which one of
Shapiro's formaldehyde-exposed informants "takes the logic of bodily reasoning to its conclusion: if wounding intimates the source of harm, then

death will surely disclose its ultimate truth."[15] Being tethered in this way to the inevitability of atmospheric death, or death due to environmental illness that is caused just by living where you live, is a way that SE Texans deal with living in a necropastoral machine.

In the necropastoral machine of SE Texas, it is statistically unlikely to avoid cancer. The disease is so commonplace (considerably higher than the national average) that its presence has become wrapped in the regional folkloric tradition; how cancer inevitably appears in one's family is a familiar hard-luck story.[16] It is intergenerational, starting with the mid-twentieth-century mesothelioma/asbestosis stories that resulted in lawsuits against oil and construction companies in the 1990s. Many of the folks at the cancer ward and elsewhere felt that these lawsuits did little to permanently alter the labor conditions through which workers were infected, including exposure via industrial boilers, turbines, pumps, and pipe insulation. The details of the cancer hard-luck story find themselves, in the twenty-first century, as comfortably settled into the reality of inevitability that positions illnesses like cancer as the event that waits somewhere along the path of every life, biding its time. Cancer here is an event that has seeped into the air, water, food, bodies succumbing to the disease in ways that escape the obscured causal conditions of late industrial consequence, "conditions that cultivate a will not to know, not to engage, not to experiment."[17] Cancer is no longer only an affliction of the poor, although the poor continue to die of it in higher numbers. It is now a mode, and so its experiential qualities are shared. They circulate as stories and repeat as repertoires; they fill medical waiting rooms with expertly performed tales of sickness, comparing ailments and side effects and severities. How a tumor was discovered, the ominous or apathetic way in which the doctor gave the diagnosis, the intensities of chemo and radiation treatments, the remoteness of one's living situation and proximity to treatment facilities, the insane costs of care and the wiliness of insurance companies, what the body does now that it has been besieged, the genealogy of sickness in one's family, the fear of death.

The biocultural event of cancer can also be seen as an affective public of caregivers, sufferers, and mourners.[18] However, the ways it is encountered are by no means universal.[19] In SE Texas, the structure of care around cancer is not necessarily characterized through a feeling of optimism; or, at least, the trappings of optimism are peripheral to the central element of the event, which is suffering. It is, for many of the cancer patients I spoke with, a structure of care divorced from the tether of hope. Again and again, witnesses to the cancer event in SE Texas told me that it was only getting worse, not only in their bodies but in the community. They would give me percentages from various sources assuring me that soon the whole world would die of cancer. "Eighty-eight percent of us! Heard that on my radio this morning," said Mr. Lambert, a patient and retired botanist. He smiled and winked and shook his head in bewilderment as he stood to leave the waiting room for his appointment with the oncologist. He turned back and looked at me with a sad grin on his face to see whether that number had registered.

When I was told stories of cancer by the old-timers at the Texas Oncology–Beaumont Mamie McFaddin Ward Cancer Center—some of whom were there as patients and some as volunteers, sitting together in the waiting room doing puzzles around a table—they almost always made sure to preface the telling with a statement that situated the present as having succumbed to seepage. Mr. Lambert came to sit in the lobby of the center most days, regardless of whether he was being seen by his oncologist. He told me about the days before "it got into the air." He assisted an expert tree specialist brought over from Germany during the height of the pine beetle scourge[20] that afflicted SE Texas's Piney Woods in the mid-twentieth century, and remembered days before the air and the forests were sick. A good friend of his who suffered from chronic respiratory issues had been told by a doctor, off the record, that if he wanted his lung problems to go away, he had to move up above one of the farm-to-market roads north of Jasper County somewhere. This road was evidently the boundary at which air became breathable again, outside the long shadow of the refineries that circled the southern half of the SE Texan perimeter. The man's friend had taken the doctor's advice, and "sure enough, his breathing got better and he didn't have any trouble afterward."

Another story that came up on multiple occasions at the center seemed to stand for how the shock of sickness emerging in the community was excessive, off the charts, exuberant beyond reason. Hearing it, you could almost sense a pride taken in its tragedy, a detailing of the ways in which the community itself reared back against the powers that asked them to fall in line, take a number, and wait their turn. The gist of the story was this: In the summer of 2002, a man from Vidor murdered a Beaumont lawyer whose firm refused to represent him in an asbestos poisoning case.[21] The Vidor man, an elderly nursing-home patient suffering from some form of senility or dementia as well as mesothelioma, returned to the law office after being refused representation and murdered one of the attorneys with a shotgun that he pulled from a box on his lap. As it turned out, the murdered man was not the attorney who had refused him service, but rather was his partner at the firm. The murder was treated as a case of mistaken identity, and all the more tragic for being so. The murdered-lawyer story leaves the teller and their audience in a place of confoundedness—what to do with the information that many people are sick—and the functionality of dealing with the necropastoral event is left open.

Casino Light

Quite a few of the patients in the cancer center spent their time across the border in Louisiana, gambling at the casinos. This was a major element of conversation in the waiting room—where you had been to gamble, if you had lost, how long you spent there, how incredible the deals were that they sent you in the mail, and how you could just forget your pain and your situation for a time and engage in a different activity. What I came to realize was that the casino was also a way of dealing with control in the larger context of people feeling that their lives were spinning out, beyond the limits of what could be dealt with, and that the gambling industry, whose billboards seemed to absorb all the light and gloss into the strange flickering eyes of the models depicted on them, funneled the untethered futures of the necropastoral machine into their rooms, where time doesn't exist.

The rural casino is marked mostly by the blatancy of its composition. Delta Downs, the casino where I spent the most time, lay just off I-10 in Vinton, Louisiana, about a forty-five-minute drive over the border from Beaumont. Built as a racetrack in 1973, it was set back in an unlikely, depressed neighborhood of dilapidated tract homes, shining there like a blighted oasis. Its parking lot was vast. The interior stunk of cigarettes, buffet meats, and unidentifiable puddings with Nilla Wafer crusts. The buffet catered to a variety of palates. Besides the attempt at regional fare (stagnant gumbos, shrimp étouffées), there were variations on ambrosia—an obscure mid-twentieth-century dinner party dessert—such as Watergate Salad, a pistachio pudding filled with pineapples and marshmallows. There was a faded sheen to the columns and mirrors, a depressed Vegas covered in a film of dust. A severity in the fluorescence laid bare each object and body, every flaw revealed. The elderly frequented Delta Downs; it was not the playground of drunken bachelorette parties or boys' night chaos. There was no cavorting, no intoxicated whooping of youth. The garish feel of the place clashed with its clientele, like a Depression-era Dorothea Lange photography exhibition in a funhouse: realism splashed with pop art in a willfully anachronistic portrait. Rows and rows of old folks sat connected to their machines, some with an umbilical cord–like device attached to the console itself—a card on a chain inserted into the slot. Their vulnerabilities flickered beneath the violently pastel lighting and glow that gave the place an atmosphere of desperate glitz. The way their lives loomed in their faces, the practiced scowl set like stone, backlit by neon. A grimacing lady in a walker slowly edging toward the buffet, traversing a scene adorned with animatronic parrots in plastic palm trees and soundtracked by whatever satellite radio station produces mid-1990s alternative radio staples along-side contemporary auto-tuned country. The machines themselves created looping aural fields that played against the backdrop of sound, clashing with it at intervals, constantly resetting. It was a wonder how the sense of calm, even apathy, prevailed amid this soundscape. The soundtrack to a Wizard of Oz slot machine cackled at the indifference; long-dead Marga-ret Hamilton as the Wicked Witch mocked their inevitable failures ("I'll get you, my pretty"), which was met with no change in the deadpan. The clanging of bells, the slide whistle of failure, and crunchy digitized fanfares were all wasted on the set stares.

As Natasha Dow Schüll has noted, frequent machine gamblers are not necessarily "playing to win."[22] That approach is found in the naiveté of the novice, optimistic in a new venture of chance. Seasoned gamblers situate themselves differently in relation to chance and its spaces; some navigate a kind of addiction—one that entrances them in the machinic activity and repetition of the gambling console, feeding their drive. Schüll character-izes the addicted machine gambler as playing within a modified death-drive framework: "It is not that the addict desires death as such . . . but that she desires release from the perturbing contingencies and uncertainties of existence."[23] They have perhaps chuckled once or twice at the cartoon impositions of the machines, but now, their poise seems to suggest, is not the time for laughter. Either we have passed the point at which this was fun, or we came here to suffer from the start. The jackpot is notional, the colors and sounds distracting. We come here to play the slots, to tune out to the patterns at work here, to cocoon ourselves in the "rinding up" of habits that these relationships engender.[24] The rest is noise.

The gamblers came as hunting clubs, taxidermy clubs in RealTree vests emblazoned with their club logos, church groups freshly back from a cruise with tropical-themed crucifix T-shirts and orthopedic beach sandals. They ate at the buffets. They were sent vouchers to stay in the hotel rooms and attend the races. They were sent pamphlets depicting young, apparently wealthy, and cosmopolitan people smiling beatifically at blackjack tables. A fair percentage of them were in wheelchairs or Rascal scooter, or they had oxygen tanks, or both. They were practically all smoking, oxygen tank or no. There was live music in the evenings. They danced carefully, or sat at the tables, bobbing their heads along to the slick band doing country standards in a style that wouldn't be out of place on *The Voice*. The casino depicted something, a composition of flashing lights and a maddening aural field of repeating musical phrases and sound effects. It was a meeting place of kitschy design and finely tuned practicality. Every machine rang out on a manic loop, contributing to the cacophony: "A thousand electronic ringtone-like bleeps and bells—the sound of the ceaseless slots—replace clock time and the shift from diurnal to nocturnal life with an unremitting temporality of the ever present."[25] Digitized voices from the machines' characters came in a variety of strange stereotypes that encouraged, scolded, or mocked. They might have a three-second repertoire of movement that engages at a moment of loss or victory: stirring a cauldron, spinning a lasso, pulling a switch that sends a trolley over the cliff, the leopard leaping from the undergrowth. There were cowboys whooping as the stampede starts again ("Heeeere we go, y'all!"), witch doctors cackling at failure, Easter Island Moai who unlock doors in an affectless baritone. A bikini-clad woman blows a kiss and the heart that issues from her mouth sets the loop in motion again. There were five-second jingles and the sounds of explosions overlaid with the *ka-ching* of the money drawer, the sound of coins clattering.

Being in the casino was bearing witness to a vulnerability on display; seeing people whose very being seemed raw or wounded or scorched, especially at sunrise, when the daylight flooded in and embarrassed the spectacle in morning. Then the effects of the lights were not as intense; the scene was more exposed, somehow guilty. Many sat at the same machine through the night and could not be bothered to stop for breakfast. They looked unwilled in the absorption of their practices. Some of them had little fetishes or lucky bits of random matter lined up along the video poker machines, dolls or action figures or old matchbooks. They executed hand gestures, flitting their fingers about in front of the screen or waving in a controlled motion: up, left, down, up, left, down. Then they pulled the crank or pressed the Bet button. These gestures brought luck; they were brought off with precision and seemed to want something. They seemed to want to reduce the chances of failure, pulling the possibility of failure from the very air: "The control they experience, constricted as it may be, affords them a chance to change their relationship to loss—not by stopping or reversing it but by performing it themselves."[26] The algorithms of the pseudorandom number generators would be dazzled for a moment, perhaps, their efficiency clouded by this ritual. I saw a woman cock her head to one side and lift one hand while pulling deeply from a cigarette as if to say, "What does it matter?" There was a shared affect: it felt like a bodily knowledge that one was exposed, one was making oneself known in this display. They labored at the machines, their bodies at work for a purpose that was never quite worked out. Once, I was in the casino with the landlord. He noticed me staring and elbowed me in the ribs, laughing: "They ought to walk around with 'Fuck Me' written on their forehead!" "Hey that one was rough," he said, as an elderly gambler limped past. A silence started to spread between us as gambler after gambler walked or scootered to the restroom. Mockery refused to encompass the feeling of the place; incredulity gave way to exhaustion. We parted ways, almost as though we had together committed some indiscretion.

Because maybe it is tough to sit with the stories and the building of character that emerges in such a place, stories in which often very poor people save up their pennies to play the machines every week, blow their SSI checks on a few pulls of a lever, eat one of their only square meals of the week at the casino buffet, and come back to do it all again the next day. It struck me as similar to the relationship to cancer. Throwing oneself into chance in a way that knows, at the end of the day, the "house" always wins. It might not make sense to try to get to the bottom of some set of underlying reasons why people gamble, but instead to tune in to people under a shared feeling, a composition that they remain wrapped within, might not be able to disconnect from, or in whose processes of manipulation they might not even actively participate. As Schüll observes, gamblers stuck in "the zone" present a deep portrait: "What clues to collective predicaments and preoccupations might we find in this solitary, driven form of existence, caught between the everyday world and the otherworldly state of the zone? . . . It becomes possible to track how shared social conditions and normative behavioral ideals contribute to shaping gambling addicts' seemingly aberrant 'machine lives,' and to discern in those lives a kind of immanent critique of broader discontents."[27] This last speculation is important, because it asks us to consider whether there is a moment in which the accrual of a shared feeling, like exhaustion or cynicism, might generate a different relationship to the ill effects of capitalism, such as a gambling addiction or a funneling through the inhuman process of cancer treatment. In the moment of pressing the Play button, a life exposes itself to a definite possibility. In the casino, it was as if losing in there might protect us from losing out here, an arcane contingency plan in which "machine-accelerated speed is a way to run ahead of the surprise and catch moments of chance—a way to be in charge of chance."[28]

One summer, Danny and I were staying with his parents (the landlord and Deb) in Kirbyville. They lived on a rural highway, the sound of eighteen-wheelers coming in waves, punctuating the underlying hum of cicadas. The call of the casino had a different effect there than it might in an urban center. It was like a beacon whose signal reached out into the darkness and drabness of the refinery zones, the depressed Piney Woods and backwaters. It was the one thing to do. We noticed it in the excess of commercials for the nearby Louisiana casinos on TV: Delta Downs, Coushatta, L'Auberge, Harrah's, or the Golden Nugget. We noted the lines of cars in the casino parking lots, RVs and pickups pouring out into the street, overwhelming the small neighborhoods. The casino billboards on the highways featuring a glowing Terry Bradshaw or advertising some "blast from the past" concert, 1970s FM-radio greats like .38 Special or Bachman-Turner Overdrive, were vivid against the austere backdrop of scorched loblolly pines and refinery complexes. Gambling addictions ran in Danny's dynastic Texan family, among other peccadilloes mentioned in hushed asides around campfires or when photo albums were dusted off, and we treated these habits with suspicion and a little pity. But time in the country propels the body into things. We were curious to see how his family spent their evenings; we were under the thrall of profound boredom after just a week of wandering about looking for night herons.

One early morning, one of Deb's older sisters, Aunt June, called up and asked if we would accompany her to Delta Downs. She had recently been widowed, and we had been seeing more of her. She was hungry for talk, for company. She treated us with an almost professional courtesy reserved for salesmen of a bygone era. She referred to us as "the boys" in a conspiratorial way, like we were rare birds. There was something practiced in it, a distance in the courtesy. This was that Texan politesse, that sociality in which what might elsewhere be mistaken as coldness or distance passes comfortably as a measured and polite care. People were giving you your space, and that was to be commended.

Aunt June changed once she entered the doors of Delta. She turned off conversation, spent the day smoking Monarchs and not budging from her machine. She didn't drink alcohol, barely bothering to wave off the bright waitresses who paraded about in a mania, impossibly kind in this mind-bending chaos. After some hours we ran into Bug, another aunt; it was a common occurrence for the ten siblings to run into each other in the casino. She was on her way out, having spent the morning. Aunt June and Bug both had a problem with gambling that fluctuated in intensity. They had a ritual of greeting each other in a sidelong fashion, both in their own ways—jokes building up behind their eyes. Bug with a little twinkle and an open-mouthed smile. Aunt June all business, purse on lap, sat erect at the machine, mouth tight and making little grunting sounds of certainty, punctuating the progress of the machine's beeps and flashes, secure in its little functions of swindling and inhabited by its strange avatars. We left with Bug.

It wasn't until the following morning that Aunt June stopped back at our place, fatigued and resigned. She had been in the casino for twenty-four hours. She had lost quite a bit of money. She said she hadn't moved all night and hadn't taken a hotel room or eaten anything or drank any water. She just sat there smoking and hitting buttons, not even one of the all-nighters with the figurines or hand-wavers. No colorful visors or fun church-club T-shirts. No enjoyment taken in the gambling. Just a perpetual duel with the machines, a tempering of the aleatory. It wasn't the first time Aunt June had spent all night in the casino; Deb had told us about another of her benders at Harrah's in New Orleans, when June had returned to their hotel room in the morning, spent and defeated. It was just after her husband had died, a long and painful struggle with leukemia. Deb described Aunt June as appearing to have shrunk overnight and changed color. She sat dejected in a chair before them, exposed to them, the composition of her. Here I am. Here is what has become of me. Deb said: "She was green, like money."

Deb's cancer continued to spread. After her final chemo and radiation treatments, when she had finally decided to seek treatment in Houston, a tumor was found in her brain. Surgery was performed, and the tumor was removed. After that, they did gamma knife radiation treatment to remove some smaller lesions on her brain. Even months after the treatments and surgeries, Deb hadn't bounced back to her former self. She lay on the couch all day, hooked up to her oxygen machine, watching TV. She no longer slept in her bedroom, feeling that the bed was too high up for her. She stopped watching the news, keeping the TV on the Game Show Network or on a program about rescuing manatees. Her family tried to get her to perform even the slightest exercises, like raising her arms or legs. The doctors gave her the "If you don't use it, you lose it" speech and referred her to a palliative care team. She said she wasn't ready for hospice, and her oncologist agreed. He said that hospice care was reserved for people who only had about six months or less to live, and she probably had more time than that. She lived in an in-between state between active life and death—her family said they were already mourning her loss, since the Deb they knew was no longer there. Her many siblings called less often, and conversation mostly stopped. They knew they would likely soon have to mourn her for real, and this felt like the first stages.

Deb's family and I sat around a fire pit while Deb lay inside. We made shrimp creole, her favorite dish, and she joined us briefly on the patio to eat before saying she felt too tired and had to go back inside using her walker. We watched the sun set and traded stories about her; the others played songs on their phones that reminded them of her, her favorite songs, compiling a funeral playlist that they'd play at the party she insisted they have after she'd gone. She wanted gardenias planted around her grave. The family had lived through Hurricane Rita back in 2005 in this tiny house, one of the most severe hurricanes in world history. The landlord had refused to evacuate, and they soldiered it out in the hallway for twelve hours. At the time, both of the landlord's parents were still living and hooked up to oxygen. At one point, the landlord said: "That wind was a hundred miles per hour for about twelve hours, with intense gusting. We thought at one point the roof would come off. I looked at Daddy, and he looked at me, and I said, 'I just don't know.' We thought maybe that was it." They reflected about how afterward the power didn't come back for two weeks, and the generator saved their lives. A massive oak had fallen onto the house, nearly splitting the roof. The area was never the same, and each subsequent hurricane seemed to keep it in its sagging state. Deb's daughter Holly, herself a cancer survivor at age thirty-nine, said: "I think that cancer is a lot like a hurricane. It comes through and ruins everything, and even when it's gone, the damage has been done, like with mom. I think it just leaves you damaged." I reflected on this idea—that cancer is like a hurricane. That life lived at the level of throwing oneself repeatedly into intense encounters of the body and the environment becomes a way of being in the world, being a character in a story about grappling with life at different levels, and of life not letting up.

Deb on the Couch

Cancer called me back to the Big Thicket three years later, in 2018. I sat with Deb's family as she came to her final days and died at home. Lulled into an unconscious state by liquid morphine, her breaths becoming more and more spaced apart, her inhalations a jolting hitch. We played her favorite songs, 1970s rock and 1980s ballads that I associate with getting my hair cut in the mall as a kid. "What a Fool Believes" by the Doobie Brothers, "Sailing" by Christopher Cross, "Mandolin Rain" by Bruce Hornsby and the Range, "Human" by the Human League—the kind of ballad in which a searing falsetto or an overwrought, soulful delivery ravages you but you are laughing at its reaches, through tears.

Cancer had left her months ago, the oncologists agreed, but the damage done by the treatments and the worsening COPD left her with one lung totally collapsed and the other at one-eighth capacity, they estimated. I waited on the screened-in porch with some other visitors while her family sat by her hospice bed, Danny holding her hand and telling her it was okay to go.

At the moment of death, the air is loaded with the feeling of signs and everything is taken as an event. Uncle Butch called us in after it was over, and we walked toward the door. One of the feral bobtail cats that lived outside, what Deb used to call the "woodpile cats" (naming an entire lit-ter of them after serial killers: Bundy, Dahmer, Gacy, Ripper) had killed a blood-red male cardinal and was ripping it apart at the threshold. The bird seemed to have expired when Deb did. This cat, Bundy, was the last of the woodpile cats—the others had died or disappeared over the years. Deb used to catalog their demises—Gacy "went and got his-self killed out on that highway," she'd say. Dahmer fought an owl—"He was mean but that owl was meaner." Ripper just vanished. Once, the cats had cornered a beaver. The cardinal was the final gift of some inscrutable initiatory rite.

The buzzards would come down and wait for the woodpile cats to walk away from their kills. We saw one dragging Gacy's entrails across the high-way like a malicious game, and Deb had laughed darkly at this final insult. I tried to reason with them about the cats, about how outdoor cats decimate bird populations and always end up dead. But Deb laughed at me and said, in her deliberate rasp, "Survival of the fittest."

There was no point in explaining natural selection—in the Kirbyville zone, this was a stuck ecology—where the effect of the cat was a resignation, a long-forgotten impingement, a nasty bit of nature folding out and letting outliers in to collect whatever spoils they could manage. There was no such thing as invasive, introduced—man's effects were not an outrage; they were already folded into the coming undone of the social fabric that is the provenance of SE Texas's hard-luck ideology, its great advantage over the hand-wringing of good liberalism. Conservatism (from which the hard-luck story draws, but it is not consumed by) sees the potential end of the line, and its comportment of poetics is based around warning others away from that end or by, in the case of Deb's libertarian sister Poodle, preparing for it in earnest. Deb was, of course, a staunch Democrat, fairly rare for a white woman in SE Texas, but the pull of the place after her whole life there acted upon her, just like it acted upon everything. She'd share posts on Facebook from the "Being Liberal" page, and for her there was no smugness to it. It was a flag of difference stabbed down into the dirt of the void. It was an "I'm here." She wore a Black Lives Matter shirt in the hospital. It was a way of establishing a boundary right away from certain types of talk. She was a woman of grand gestures. That dead cardinal was a fanfare out. It was the last bird I ever saw in Kirbyville.

Poodle was there at the end, crying for Deb. When Deb got sick, Poodle started bringing over herbs and supplements to fight cancer. She would come into the health food store while I was working and hand me a list. Deb was wary of these moves—Poodle had done the same with their mother back in the 1990s when she got sick. She had made their mother drink carrot juice and shark fin, and she had prayed over her when no one was listening. She'd wave her hands over her the way people wave their hands in front of slot machines to charm them into hitting. Deb said her mother had turned orange and died anyway. Poodle believed in the invocation of the unseen and the manipulation of materials to bring the body back. They were two completely oppositional forms of pragmatism.

After Deb's mind started to slip, Poodle began to show up more and more often. Holly caught her trying to bring in a man from the Southern Baptist church in Kirbyville and had to explain to her that Deb was not religious, had two gay children, and didn't want some fire-and-brimstone conservative preacher around her. Poodle backed off a bit after that, but she stuck around, texting their other libertarian sister to give her updates about how it was all being handled. Poodle slipped into the character of the burdensome aunt, standing off to the side and shouting orders while everyone ignored her.

And everyone else became characters too: mourners, those who sat by and cried, the ones who paced back and forth and talked nonstop, the ones who couldn't bear it and stood outside—and the ones who never came in the first place, even though Deb had taken in their children when they had dropped them off in her driveway to go join cults in Idaho, to dry off in some shack somewhere, to meet up with secret lovers in country highway motels with names like Piney Woods Inn and Big Thicket Motel and Golden Triangle and Bayou Rest. Some came in and wept around her, and some stayed away. And in the middle of it all, she went into the darkness, bigger than life, the character of who she was and who she had become accruing around her.

Her mind hadn't just gone—people said she hadn't been herself for a long time. There were many Debs in the end. There was the weathered, sense-making version; the one who got angry; and the one who was in complete chaos. Just as there were many ends to her life. There was the diagnosis, the crippling chemo, the surgery that ended her mobility, the unraveling of her mind, and then her body's death.

After her body's death, the impingements of place started to reassert themselves. The first was the sudden arrival of the mustached man from the funeral home who came to collect her body. He must have been in his early eighties, in a crumpled dark suit, wheeling a gurney. His presence, the character of him, immediately changed the house into the atmosphere of a funeral home. He was all Texan politesse: speaking softly only to the men and going about the business of wrapping her and zipping her into a body bag with delicacy, not a movement wasted, like a songbird at the feeder. After getting Deb's body onto the gurney, he strapped her in with restraints and calmly told us all a story, at very low volume, but loud enough for all to hear, about how there had been incidents in the past in which the bodies had been damaged in car accidents on the way back to the funeral home, left "too damaged to display." So "now I strap 'em in real good," he said. There was no pleasure taken by him in the relaying of this information. It was something that had to be said. The men nodded politely at this macabre, plain truth—the matter-of-fact delivery was placating. It was helpful for us to have been told this. He smiled at us wanly, shook the men's hands, and calmly wheeled Deb off into the night, totally alone.

The hospice nurses sent a minister over again, after Deb was gone. He caught the landlord in a moment of weakness. Deb hadn't wanted a funeral; she had wanted a party. But the young minister, who arrived in a car marked with the logo of the hospice, Affinity, convinced him otherwise. I noticed skull tattoos up and down the minister's arms, which he had covered in a white button-down, but you could see through—one of the many reformed sinners who end up ministering to the youth of SE Texas in summer retreats and Bible study. Finally, Deb's children put their foot down, and the minister backed off, saying, "To be honest, when I saw you folks, I had you pegged as *memorial people*." This was a way of saying he recognized difference when he saw it. Memorial people don't send their dead off with the Lord.

In fact, the only people to speak at Deb's funeral were queer. Her nephew, Holly's best friend, Danny, and myself at the burial, which took place at the family cemetery next to their home. Danny made rainbow ribbons and blue-and-yellow ribbons to signify the colors of the Human Rights Campaign. We laughed at the reorientation this brought us— outside, we would never wear rainbows; in fact we loathed them and found the politics associated with most Pride events to be reactionary. But, like the queer articulation of self in SE Texas, we realized that there—in Kirbyville, in a funeral home the color of sand with art on the walls showing sad cows and empty pastures and Jesus bearing down upon you with beautiful eyes, where we filled a bowl marked "Equality and pride were issues dear to Deb. Wear one if you wish" with rainbow ribbons—what queer means became something different. In Kirbyville, the rainbow lapel pin was not a symbol of "homonormativity"; such words don't even make it out of your mouth there in the same way. It was a recognizable form of difference that disrupted the already troubled ordinary. As did the Barack Obama and Jimmy Carter and John Lennon quotes on the funeral program that the funeral director was loath to print.

The funeral was itself a portrait of severity, although it wasn't without laughter. But the laughter was incredulous; it came in stifled outbursts in this beige-carpeted room with new pews and Kenny Rogers's "Through the Years" piped in over the loudspeaker on repeat—a mistake the funeral director didn't know he was making. Bug came in crying with a box of Ding Dongs. Deb had been her lifeline. She went up to the landlord, saying, "She loved these." It dawned on the entire room simultaneously that her intention was to place them in the casket. "Please don't," he said. Later, I noticed someone had snuck in a Hershey bar. Deb had loved chocolate, but the question became: Did it warrant her taking it into the afterlife?

Afterward, at the family cemetery, we all gathered and told stories about Deb, some funny, some hard luck and sad, some just real. One woman, a friend of Deb's from way back in her wild days, tried to say a few words, but she couldn't seem to put anything together: "Well, Deb and I were friends, and I moved away, but we talked . . . and I did end up moving back. . . ."

my husband worked, and um . . . well . . ." The story stalled, and everything just hung there. The eulogy form wasn't happening with her. The landlord thanked her brusquely, and she went away.

Deb's eldest living sister, Aunt June, stood up with the help of her daughter and came to the front, standing beside the casket. I had never seen her cry (I don't think any of us had), and the effect was a total rupture from the proceedings. She was one of the toughest human beings any of us knew, the widow of the Beaumont police chief and an expert on geography and the kind of facts I call "Texana." Her weeping came out in harsh croaks, her oxygen tank making the periodic hissing noise. You could see that Deb's death had devastated her. She seemed to have grown a bit older and a bit smaller during the funeral. It hurt to watch—you felt it in your chest. She said, as time stopped, "When I think of my sister Deb, I see a little girl with her hair in her face, hiding pain."

Notes

Introduction

1. Peacock, *Nature Lover's Guide to the Big Thicket*, 1.

2. "What Is the Golden Triangle of Texas?," Gobeau, accessed May 12, 2022, https://www.gobeau.co/post/what-is-the-golden-triangle-of-texas.

3. "Beaumont's 135-foot Alligator," Beaumont Convention and Visitors Bureau, accessed May 12, 2022, https://www.beaumontcvb.com/things-to-do/roadside -attractions/giant-alligator/.

4. Reed and Bialecki, "Introduction to Special Section 1."

5. Bauman, *Story, Performance, and Event*.

6. McCormack, "Atmospheric Things and Circumstantial Excursions," 605.

7. Berlant, *Cruel Optimism*, 199.

8. Marisol de la Cadena's ontological concept of multiplicity, elaborated in *Earth Beings: Ecologies of Practice across Andean Worlds*.

9. De la Cadena, "The Politics of Modern Politics Meets Ethnographies of Excess through Ontological Openings."

10. See, for example, Benedict, *The Chrysanthemum and the Sword*; Mead, *And Keep Your Powder Dry*; and Gorer, *The People of Great Russia*.

11. See the special section on anthropology and character in *Social Anthropology* 26, no. 2 (2018), edited by Adam Reed and Jon Bialecki.

12. I borrow the term *figuration* from Donna Haraway, who uses it throughout her work and elucidates it most clearly her 2000 lecture "Birth of the Kennel," accessed April 12, 2018, from Latvijas Antropologu Biedrība / Latvian Anthropological Association, http://antropologubiedriba.wikidot.com/haraway-lecture-cyborgs.

13. Here I am drawing from Auerbach, *Mimesis.*

14. Candea, *Comparison in Anthropology.*

15. Bonney, *Big Thicket Guidebook.*

16. Ogden, *Swamplife.*

17. Lingeman, *Small Town America,* 103.

18. Pittman, *The Stories of I. C. Eason, King of the Dog People.*

19. Chambers, "Goodbye God, I'm Going to Texas."

20. "Beaumont," Tour Texas, accessed April 4, 2022, https://www.tourtexas.com /destinations/beaumont.

21. This thread begins in the early 1990s with Susan Harding's seminal essay "Representing Fundamentalism: The Problem of the Repugnant Cultural Other." It is continued in various disciplines, throughout the 1990s and 2000s by anthropologists (Hartigan, *Racial Situations;* Hartigan, *Odd Tribes*) and sociologists (Newitz and Wray, *White Trash;* Wray, *Not Quite White*) and has reached best-seller status in works for a more general readership in recent years (Isenberg, *White Trash;* Vance, *Hillbilly Elegy;* Hochschild, *Strangers in Their Own Land*).

22. I am not saying that there no Indigenous people in the figure of the rural Other. SE Texas was stolen from the Atakapa-Ishak, Indigenous peoples of the Southeastern Woodlands whose Western and Eastern bands were known as the Sunset and Sunrise People, respectively. The Big Thicket was home to the Western Atakapa Nial, or Panther Band, of the Atakapa. *Atakapa* is an exonym, the Chocktaw word for *man-eater,* apparently a reference to the Atakapa-Ishak's cannibalism practices. Their autonym is *Ishak,* "the people." The border between what are now Louisiana and Texas was inhabited by the Tsikip, or Heron Band (Opelousa), of the Eastern Atakapa, who painted their legs and feet black like the heron during rituals of mourning.

23. A Confederate flag still flies at Evadale High School in Jasper County, as well as appearing on its gymnasium wall and football field; its mascot is the Rebel. Accounts of the Vidor highway sign's existence and tenure vary—some insist that it was on display until the 1980s; some say it was taken down in the 1970s. Others claim it never existed and support this with the fact that there are "no known photographs" of the sign. Yet many people I spoke to over the course of my time in SE Texas remember it clearly. Collective memory distorts consensus—the sign is lost in the miasmic fog of Vidor's misremembering.

24. Stewart called this repertoire "back-talk" in *A Space on the Side of the Road.*

25. Benjamin, *Illuminations.*

26. Stewart, *A Space on the Side of the Road.*

27. Fortun, "Ethnography in Late Industrialism."

28. Of those who voted: a fraction of the population.

29. Shapiro, "Attuning to the Chemosphere."

30. Burke, "The Cajun Navy."

31. Samuels, "Dan Patrick Says."

32. These later moved to 8chan and then 8kun. QAnon is a "*quasi*-secular millenarian" in the sense that it is entrenched in a cross-pollinating relationship with Christian fundamentalism and only partially committed to eschatology as such, yet deeply informed by its mythos. One podcast calls this "conspirituality." See Derek Beres, Matthew Remski, and Julian Walker, *Conspirituality*, https://conspirituality.buzzsprout.com/1875696. The identity of the figure of Q is theorized to be various people, most notably the owner of 8kun, Jim Watkins, and Jason Gelinas of New Jersey, who is supposedly behind QMap.pub and a new platform for Q believers called Armor of God. "Q Clearance Patriot" is a reference to the highest level of security clearance at the US Department of Energy. Q clearance has a long history within American conspiracy theory circles as a prestigious title for those with access to the most highly classified material. See also Nagle, *Kill All Normies*.

33. One origin point for Euro-American conspiracy theory is the publication of *The Protocols of the Elders of Zion* in 1903.

34. Lepselter, *The Resonance of Unseen Things*.

35. "QAnon Key Figure Revealed as Financial Information Security Analyst from New Jersey," Logically, September 10, 2020, https://www.logically.ai/articles/qanon-key-figure-man-from-new-jersey. The website was Qmap.pub; another website where the drops were uploaded is Qanon.pub.

36. *Deep hanging out* is a term often attributed to Clifford Geertz but possibly first coined by Renato Rosaldo.

Chapter One. The Strange Time of Hard-Luck Stories

Excerpts from this chapter were published as "Time Gets Strange: Texan Hard-Luck Stories," in *Feelings of Structure*, edited by Yoke-Sum Wong and Karen Engle (Montreal: McGill-Queen's University Press, 2018), 106–15.

1. Bauman, *Story, Performance, and Event*.

2. See, e.g., "Beaumont TX Crime Rate 1999–2018," MacroTrends, accessed May 3, 2022, https://www.macrotrends.net/cities/us/tx/beaumont/crime-rate-statistics; "The 10 Most and Least Educated Cities in America," Forbes, September 16, 2014, https://www.forbes.com/pictures/fjle45iglg/no-1-least-educated-city/?sh=3bef413968ce.

3. Johnson, *Just Queer Folks*; Ferguson, "Sissies at the Picnic."

4. The rice fields were originally farmed by the Japanese Mayumi family, who purchased the land in 1905. The road abutting their property was called "Jap Road" until repeated petitions by the Anti-Defamation League saw Jefferson County change the name to Boondocks Road in 2004. Klicker, "A Road in Texas."

5. Stewart, *A Space on the Side of the Road*, 51.

6. Berlant, *Cruel Optimism*.

7. Linguists refer to this as the "punctual whenever." See, for example, Montgomery and Kirk, "'My Mother, Whenever She Passed Away, She Had Pneumonia.'"

8. Blanchfield, *Proxies*, 72.

9. Jones was technically an honorary Vidorian. He was born in the Big Thicket proper, in the unincorporated town of Saratoga, Texas, in Hardin County.

10. Lemanager, *Living Oil*.

11. The nature of Texan character is autodidactic, rebellious, and anti-institutional.

12. Etienne-Gray, "Higgins, Pattillo (1863–1995)."

13. Gulf Oil and Texaco are now merged under Chevron.

14. Malewitz, "A Deadly Industry."

15. Kristeva, *Powers of Horror*; Douglas, *Purity and Danger*.

16. Ching, "The Possum, the Hag, and the Rhinestone Cowboy," 118.

17. Kristeva, *Powers of Horror*, 71, emphasis mine.

18. Douglas, *Purity and Danger*.

19. Bakhtin, *Rabelais and His World*, 317.

20. Ghansah, "A Most American Terrorist."

21. Agee and Evans, *Let Us Now Praise Famous Men*, 9–10.

22. Bonnet, *The Infra-World*.

23. Ching, "The Possum, the Hag, and the Rhinestone Cowboy," 124.

24. This wasn't true, as I later discovered. At least one of the murderers was in fact from Jasper.

Chapter Two. The Higher the Hair, the Closer to God

Excerpts from this chapter were published as "Time Gets Strange: Texan Hard-Luck Stories," in *Feelings of Structure*, edited by Yoke-Sum Wong and Karen Engle (Montreal: McGill-Queen's University Press, 2018), 106–15.

1. Elisha, "Proximations of Public Religion."

2. Handman, *Critical Christianity*, 41.

3. I use *evangelical* here to refer to several SE Texan Christian practices, including Messianic Judaism, due to the nature of evangelism's influence over their belief structure and practices of worship.

4. Warner, "Tongues Untied."

5. Harding, *The Book of Jerry Falwell*.

6. Crawley, *Blackpentecostal Breath*.

7. Ammerman, *Bible Believers*.

8. Keane, *Christian Moderns*; Engelke, *The Problem of Presence*.

9. The current manifestation of this belief within the evolution of evangelical practice in the United States first emerged during the 1960s with the appearance of "Jesus freaks"; see Luhrmann, *When God Talks Back*.

10. Slotta, "Revelations of the World."

11. Stewart, "Worlding Refrains."

12. Schopenhauer, *The World as Will and Representation*, 19.

13. "7-CD Set," Michael S. Tyrrell, accessed May 12, 2022, http://www .michaeltyrrell.com/music/. The CDs came with an accompanying booklet detailing Tyrrell's epiphany after he was given the method of transposing music to the key of David by a stranger in an Israeli bar.

14. See, for example, "Prayer #6—Hear O Israel: Part 1," Aish, May 8, 2009, https://www.aish.com/sp/pr/48944836.html.

15. Leman, "At the YIC Blog."

16. I refer to these three salespeople as the "ladies," a group term we jokingly landed on while out to lunch, when Miss Rudie exclaimed, "It's Joey and his ladies!" much to the amusement of the rest. I find the term more appropriate than referring to them as "women" given the familiar and familial nature of our interactions and the way they carried themselves at work—with a friendly-yet-distant Texan politesse that, for me, conjured up the twentieth century and its Golden Age of Hollywood "Southern Lady" icons.

17. Boone, "Almost Heaven, Idaho, Is Almost Silent Now."

18. Bonnet, *The Infra-World*, 59.

19. Barrett, "Colloidal Silver."

Chapter Three. Queer Character and the Golden Triangle

1. Gray, Gilley, and Johnson, *Queering the Countryside*.

2. Annes and Redlin, "Coming Out and Coming Back."

3. Boellstorff, "When Marriage Falls," 234.

4. Gray, *Out in the Country*.

5. De la Cadena, *Earth Beings*, 28.

6. Manalansan, "Queer Worldings," 566.

7. Gray, Gilley, and Johnson, *Queering the Countryside*.

Chapter Four. Ringing Out

A version of the casino section of this chapter was previously published as "Casino Light," *Capacious: Journal for Emergent Affect Inquiry* 1, no. 1 (2016): 1–11.

1. Nomex is a heat-resistant synthetic fiber that was created and distributed by DuPont in the late 1960s and continues to be sold.

2. Fortun, "Ethnography in Late Industrialism," 460.

3. Povinelli, "Fires Fogs Winds."

4. Stewart, "Atmospheric Attunements"; Shapiro, "Attuning to the Chemosphere."

5. Shapiro, "Attuning to the Chemosphere," 370.

6. Nixon, *Slow Violence and the Environmentalism of the Poor*.

7. Berlant, "The Commons."

8. Burke and Mathews, "Returning to Earth," 180.

9. Shapiro, "Attuning to the Chemosphere."

10. McSweeney, *The Necropastoral*.

11. Goodman and Leatherman, *Building a New Biocultural Synthesis*.

12. Shaw and Younes, "The Most Detailed Map of Cancer-Causing Industrial Air Pollution in the U.S."

13. Berger, *After the End*, xiii.

14. McSweeney, *The Necropastoral*, 1.

15. Shapiro, "Attuning to the Chemosphere," 386.

16. "Texas Cancer Registry," accessed July 16, 2019, https://cancer-rates.info/tx/.

17. Fortun, "Ethnography in Late Industrialism," 459.

18. Burke, Kampriani, and Mathews, *Anthropologies of Cancer in Transnational Worlds*.

19. Burke and Mathews, "Returning to Earth."

20. Billings and Pase, "What Happened to the Southern Pine Beetle?"

21. Lozano, "Prominent Beaumont Lawyer Shot to Death at Firm."

22. Schüll, *Addiction by Design*.

23. Schüll, *Addiction by Design*, 223.

24. Stewart, "Atmospheric Attunements."

25. The Project on Vegas, *Strip Cultures*.

26. Schüll, *Addiction by Design*, 216.

27. Schüll, *Addiction by Design*, 190–91.

28. Schüll, *Addiction by Design*, 219.

Bibliography

Agee, James, and Walker Evans. *Let Us Now Praise Famous Men: The American Classic, in Words and Photographs, of Three Tenant Families in the Deep South.* New York: Mariner Books, 2001.

Ammerman, Nancy Tatum. *Bible Believers: Fundamentalists in the Modern World.* New Brunswick, NJ: Rutgers University Press, 1987.

Anderson, Ben. "Affective Atmospheres." *Emotion, Space and Society* 2, no. 2 (2009): 77–81.

Annes, Alexis, and Meredith Redlin. "Coming Out and Coming Back: Rural Gay Migration and the City." *Journal of Rural Studies* 28, no. 1 (2012): 56–68.

Appadurai, Arjun. "The Ghost in the Financial Machine." *Public Culture* 23, no. 3 (2011): 517–39.

Auerbach, Erich. *Mimesis: The Representation of Reality in Western Literature.* Princeton, NJ: Princeton University Press, 2013.

Bakhtin, Mikhail. *Rabelais and His World.* Bloomington: Indiana University Press, 1984.

Barrett, Stephen. "Colloidal Silver: Risk without Benefit." Quackwatch, June 27, 2021. https://quackwatch.org/related/PhonyAds/silverad/.

Bauman, Richard. *Story, Performance, and Event: Contextual Studies of Oral Narrative.* Cambridge: Cambridge University Press, 1986.

Benedict, Ruth. *The Chrysanthemum and the Sword: Patterns of Japanese Culture.* Boston: Houghton Mifflin, 1946.

Benjamin, Walter. "The Destructive Character." 1931. Translated by Edmund Jephcott. In *Selected Writings,* vol. 2, part 2: *1931–1934,* edited by Michael W. Jennings, Howard Eiland, and Gary Smith, 541–42. Cambridge, MA: Belknap Press, 1999.

Benjamin, Walter. *Illuminations: Essays and Reflections.* Translated by Harry Zohn. Edited by Hannah Arendt. Boston: Mariner Books, 2019.

Berger, James. *After the End: Representations of Post-apocalypse*. Minneapolis: University of Minnesota Press, 1999.

Berlant, Lauren. "The Commons: Infrastructures for Troubling Times." *Environment and Planning D: Society and Space* 34, no. 3 (2016): 393–419.

Berlant, Lauren. *Cruel Optimism*. Durham, NC: Duke University Press, 2011.

Berlant, Lauren. "Trump, or Political Emotions." *New Inquiry*, August 5, 2016. https://thenewinquiry.com/trump-or-political-emotions/.

Bersani, Leo. *Homos*. Cambridge, MA: Harvard University Press, 1996.

Billings, Ronald F., and Herbert A. (Joe) Pase III. "What Happened to the Southern Pine Beetle?" Forest Health, Texas A&M Forest Service, July 2010. https://tfsweb.tamu.edu/Content/Article.aspx?id=21262.

Blanchfield, Brian. *Proxies: Essays Near Knowing*. New York: Nightboat Books, 2016.

Böhme, Gernot. "Atmosphere as the Fundamental Concept of a New Aesthetics." *Thesis Eleven*, no. 36 (1993): 113–26.

Boellstorff, Tom. "When Marriage Falls: Queer Coincidences in Straight Time." *GLQ: A Journal of Gay and Lesbian Studies* 13, nos. 2–3 (2007): 227–48.

Bonnet, François J. *The Infra-World*. Translated by Amy Ireland and Robin Mackay. Falmouth, UK: Urbanomic, 2017.

Bonney, Lorraine G. *The Big Thicket Guidebook: Exploring the Backroads and History of Southeast Texas*. Denton: University of North Texas Press, 2011.

Boone, Rebecca. "Almost Heaven, Idaho, Is Almost Silent Now." *Salt Lake Tribune*, August 30, 2004. https://archive.sltrib.com/article.php?id=2400556&itype =NGPSID.

Brennan, Teresa. *The Transmission of Affect*. Ithaca, NY: Cornell University Press, 2004.

Brett, Bill. *There Ain't No Such Animal and Other East Texas Tales*. College Station: Texas A&M University Press, 1979.

Brett, Bill. *This Here's a Good'un*. College Station: Texas A&M University Press, 1983.

Brooks, Cleanth. *William Faulkner: The Yoknapatawpha Country*. Baton Rouge: Louisiana State University Press, 1963.

Burke, Monte. "The Cajun Navy: The Rescuers." Garden & Gun, April/May 2020. https://gardenandgun.com/articles/the-cajun-navy-the-rescuers/.

Burke, Nancy J., Eirini Kampriani, and Holly F. Mathews, eds. *Anthropologies of Cancer in Transnational Worlds*. London: Routledge, 2015.

Burke, Nancy J., and Holly F. Mathews. "Returning to Earth: Setting a Global Agenda for the Anthropology of Cancer." *Medical Anthropology* 36, no. 3 (2017): 179–86. https://doi.org/10.1080/01459740.2016.1255611.

Candea, Matei. *Comparison in Anthropology: The Impossible Method*. Cambridge: Cambridge University Press, 2018.

Chambers, Glenn. "'Goodbye God, I'm Going to Texas': The Migration of Louisiana Creoles of Colour and the Preservation of Black Catholic and Creole

Traditions in Southeast Texas." *Journal of Religion and Popular Culture* 26, no. 1 (2014): 124–43.

Ching, Barbara. "The Possum, the Hag, and the Rhinestone Cowboy: Hard Country Music and the Burlesque Abjection of the White Man." In *Whiteness: A Critical Reader*, edited by Mike Hill, 117–33. New York: New York University Press, 1997.

Choy, Timothy. *Ecologies of Comparison: An Ethnography of Endangerment in Hong Kong*. Durham, NC: Duke University Press, 2011.

Crawley, Ashon T. *Blackpentecostal Breath: The Aesthetics of Possibility*. New York: Fordham University Press, 2016.

Cvetkovich, Ann. *Depression: A Public Feeling*. Durham, NC: Duke University Press, 2012.

de la Cadena, Marisol. *Earth Beings: Ecologies of Practice across Andean Worlds*. Durham, NC: Duke University Press, 2015.

de la Cadena, Marisol. "The Politics of Modern Politics Meets Ethnographies of Excess through Ontological Openings." Theorizing the Contemporary, *Fieldsights*, January 13, 2014. https://culanth.org/fieldsights/the-politics-of -modern-politics-meets-ethnographies-of-excess-through-ontological -openings.

Denzin, Norman. *Interpretive Ethnography: Ethnographic Practices for the 21st Century*. Thousand Oaks, CA: Sage, 1996.

Douglas, Mary. *Purity and Danger*. London: Routledge, 1966.

Dudley, Kathryn M. *Debt and Dispossession: Farm Loss in America's Heartland*. Chicago: University of Chicago Press, 2002.

Dudley, Kathryn M. *The End of the Line: Lost Jobs, New Lives in Postindustrial America*. Chicago: Chicago University Press, 1997.

Dufrenne, Mikel. *The Phenomenology of Aesthetic Experience*. Evanston, IL: Northwestern University Press, 1973.

Dumm, Thomas. *A Politics of the Ordinary*. New York: New York University Press, 1999.

Duncan, Cynthia M. *Worlds Apart: Poverty and Politics in Rural America*. New Haven, CT: Yale University Press, 1999.

Edelman, Lee. "The Future Is Kid Stuff: Queer Theory, Disidentification, and the Death Drive." *Narrative* 6, no. 1 (1998): 18–30.

Edelman, Lee. *No Future: Queer Theory and the Death Drive*. Durham, NC: Duke University Press, 2004.

Elisha, Omri. "Faith beyond Belief: Evangelical Protestant Conceptions of Faith and the Resonance of Anti-humanism." *Social Analysis* 52, no. 1 (2008): 56–78.

Elisha, Omri. "Proximations of Public Religion: Worship, Spiritual Warfare, and the Ritualization of Christian Dance." *American Anthropologist* 119, no. 1 (2017): 74–85.

Engelke, Matthew. *The Problem of Presence: Beyond Scripture in an African Church*. Berkeley: University of California Press, 2007.

Entrikin, J. Nicholas. *The Betweenness of Place*. Baltimore, MD: Johns Hopkins University Press, 1991.

Etienne-Gray, Tracé. "Higgins, Pattillo (1863–1995)." In *Handbook of Texas*. Texas State Historical Association, 1976; updated September 16, 2020. https://www .tshaonline.org/handbook/entries/higgins-pattillo.

Fabian, Johannes. *Time and the Other: How Anthropology Makes Its Object*. New York: Columbia University Press, 2002.

Ferguson, Roderick. "Sissies at the Picnic: The Subjugated Knowledges of a Black Rural Queer." In *Feminist Waves, Feminist Generations: Life Stories from the Academy*, edited by Hokulani K. Aikau, Karla A. Erickson, and Jennifer L. Pierce, 188–96. Minneapolis: University of Minnesota Press, 2007.

Fortun, Kim. "Ethnography in Late Industrialism." *Cultural Anthropology* 27, no. 3 (2012): 446–64.

Ghansah, Rachel Kaadzi. "A Most American Terrorist: The Making of Dylann Roof." *GQ*, August 21, 2017. https://www.gq.com/story/dylann-roof-making -of-an-american-terrorist.

Goldsby, Jacqueline. *A Spectacular Secret: Lynching in American Life and Literature*. Chicago: University of Chicago Press, 2006.

Goodman, Alan H., and Thomas L. Leatherman, eds. *Building a New Biocultural Synthesis: Political-Economic Perspectives on Human Biology*. Ann Arbor: University of Michigan Press, 1998.

Gorer, Geoffrey. *The People of Great Russia: A Psychological Study*. New York: Norton, 1962.

Gray, Mary L. *Out in the Country: Youth, Media, and Queer Visibility in Rural America*. New York: New York University Press, 2009.

Gray, Mary L., Brian J. Gilley, and Colin R. Johnson, eds. *Queering the Countryside: New Frontiers in Rural Queer Studies*. New York: New York University Press, 2016.

Guattari, Félix. *The Three Ecologies*. London: Athlone, 2000.

Handman, Courtney. *Critical Christianity: Translation and Denominational Conflict in Papua New Guinea*. Berkeley: University of California Press, 2015.

Haraway, Donna J. *The Companion Species Manifesto: Dogs, People, and Significant Otherness*. Chicago: Prickly Paradigm, 2003.

Harding, Susan Friend. *The Book of Jerry Falwell: Fundamentalist Language and Politics*. Princeton, NJ: Princeton University Press, 2001.

Hartigan, John. *Odd Tribes: Toward a Cultural Analysis of White People*. Durham, NC: Duke University Press, 2005.

Hartigan, John. *Racial Situations: Class Predicaments of Whiteness in Detroit*. Princeton, NJ: Princeton University Press, 1999.

Hastrup, Kirsten. "The Ethnographic Present: A Reinvention." *Cultural Anthropology* 5, no. 1 (1990): 45–61.

Herring, Scott. *Another Country: Queer Anti-urbanism*. New York: New York University Press, 2010.

Hochschild, Arlie Russell. *Strangers in Their Own Land: Anger and Mourning on the American Right*. New York: New Press, 2016.

Hunter, James Davison. *Culture Wars: The Struggle to Define America*. New York: Basic Books, 1992.

Isenberg, Nancy. *White Trash: The 400-Year Untold History of Class in America*. New York: Penguin, 2017.

Jain, S. Lochlann. *Malignant: How Cancer Becomes Us*. Berkeley: University of California Press, 2013.

Johnson, Colin R. *Just Queer Folks: Gender and Sexuality in Rural America*. Philadelphia: Temple University Press, 2013.

Keane, Webb. *Christian Moderns: Freedom and Fetish in the Mission Encounter*. Berkeley: University of California Press, 2007.

Kirksey, Eben. *Freedom in Entangled Worlds: West Papua and the Architecture of Global Power*. Durham, NC: Duke University Press, 2012.

Klicker, Hellmut. "A Road in Texas." Japanese American Citizens League Houston Chapter. http://hirasaki.net/Family_Stories/Mayumi/Mayumi_History.htm.

Kristeva, Julia. *Powers of Horror: An Essay on Abjection*. New York: Columbia University Press, 1982.

Latour, Bruno. "An Attempt at a 'Compositionist' Manifesto." *New Literary History* 41, no. 3 (2010): 471–90.

Law, John. *After Method: Mess in Social Science Research*. London: Routledge, 2004.

Leman, Derek. "At the YIC Blog: Gematria in the New Testament." *Messianic Jewish Musings*, May 26, 2011. http://www.messianicjudaism.me/musings/2011/05/26/at-the-yic-blog-gematria-in-the-new-testament/.

Lemanager, Stephanie. *Living Oil: Petroleum Culture in the American Century*. Oxford: Oxford University Press, 2013.

Lepselter, Susan. *The Resonance of Unseen Things: Poetics, Power, Captivity, and UFOs in the American Uncanny*. Ann Arbor: University of Michigan Press, 2016.

Lingeman, Richard. *Small Town America: A Narrative History 1620–the Present*. Boston: Houghton Mifflin, 1980.

Lozano, Juan A. "Prominent Beaumont Lawyer Shot to Death at Firm." *MyPlainview*, June 13, 2002. https://www.myplainview.com/news/article/Prominent-Beaumont-lawyer-shot-to-death-at-firm-9003411.php.

Luhrmann, Tanya M. *When God Talks Back: Understanding the American Evangelical Relationship with God*. New York: Vintage, 2012.

Malewitz, Jim. "A Deadly Industry." *EHS Today*, March 31, 2015. https://www.ehstoday.com/safety/article/21916835/a-deadly-industry.

Manalansan, Martin F., IV. 2013. "Queer Worldings: The Messy Art of Being Global in Manila and New York." *Antipode* 47, no. 3 (2013): 566–79.

Mbembe, Achille. 2003. "Necropolitics." *Public Culture* 15, no. 1 (2003): 11–40.

McCormack, Derek P. 2014. "Atmospheric Things and Circumstantial Excursions." *Cultural Geographies* 21, no. 4 (2014): 605–25.

McLean, Stuart. 2009. "Stories and Cosmogonies: Imagining Creativity beyond 'Nature' and 'Culture.'" *Cultural Anthropology* 24, no. 2 (2009): 213–45.

McSweeney, Joyelle. *The Necropastoral: Poetry, Media, Occults*. Ann Arbor: University of Michigan Press, 2014.

Mead, Margaret. *And Keep Your Powder Dry: An Anthropologist Looks at America*. New York: Berghahn Books, 2000.

Mitropoulos, Angela. "'Post-factual' Readings of Neoliberalism, Before and After Trump." *Society & Space*, December 5, 2016. https://www.societyandspace .org/articles/post-factual-readings-of-neoliberalism-before-and-after -trump.

Montgomery, Michael B., and John M. Kirk. "'My Mother, Whenever She Passed Away, She Had Pneumonia': The History and Functions of *Whenever*." *Journal of English Linguistics* 29, no. 3 (2001): 234–49.

Muñoz, José Esteban. *Cruising Utopia: The Then and There of Queer Futurity*. New York: New York University Press, 2009.

Muñoz, José Esteban. *Disidentifications: Queers of Color and the Performance of Politics*. Minneapolis: University of Minnesota Press, 1999.

Nagle, Angela. *Kill All Normies: Online Culture Wars from 4chan and Tumblr to Trump and the Alt-Right*. Winchester: Zero Books, 2017.

Newitz, Annalee, and Matt Wray, eds. *White Trash: Race and Class in America*. London: Routledge, 1996.

Ngai, Sianne. *Ugly Feelings*. Cambridge, MA: Harvard University Press, 2005.

Nixon, Rob. *Slow Violence and the Environmentalism of the Poor*. Cambridge, MA: Harvard University Press, 2011.

Ogden, Laura. *Swamplife: People, Gators, and Mangroves Entangled in the Everglades*. Minneapolis: University of Minnesota Press, 2011.

Peacock, Howard. *Nature Lover's Guide to the Big Thicket*. College Station: Texas A&M University Press, 1994.

Pine, Jason. "Last Chance Incorporated." *Cultural Anthropology* 31, no. 2 (2016): 297–318.

Pittman, Blair. *The Stories of I. C. Eason, King of the Dog People*. Denton: University of North Texas Press, 1996.

Povinelli, Elizabeth. "Radical Worlds: The Anthropology of Incommensurability and Inconceivability." *Annual Review of Anthropology* 30 (2001): 319–34.

Powell, Douglas Reichert. *Critical Regionalism: Connecting Politics and Culture in the American Landscape*. Chapel Hill: University of North Carolina Press, 2007.

The Project on Vegas. *Strip Cultures: Finding America in Las Vegas*. Durham, NC: Duke University Press, 2015.

Rancière, Jacques. *Disagreement: Politics and Philosophy*. Minneapolis: University of Minnesota Press, 2004.

Rancière, Jacques. *The Intellectual and His People: Staging the People*. Vol. 2. Translated by David Fernbach. London: Verso Books, 2012.

Reed, Adam, and Jon Bialecki. "Introduction to Special Section 1: Anthropology and Character." *Social Anthropology* 26, no. 2 (2018): 159–67. https://doi.org /10.1111/1469-8676.12479.

Samuels, Alex. "Dan Patrick Says 'There Are More Important Things than Living and That's Saving This Country.'" *Texas Tribune*, April 21, 2020. https://www .texastribune.org/2020/04/21/texas-dan-patrick-economy-coronavirus/.

Schopenhauer, Arthur. *The World as Will and Representation*. Vol. 1. New York: Dover, 1966.

Schüll, Natasha Dow. "Abiding Chance: Online Poker and the Software of Self-Discipline." *Public Culture* 28, no. 3 (2016): 563–92.

Schüll, Natasha Dow. *Addiction by Design: Machine Gambling in Las Vegas*. Princeton, NJ: Princeton University Press, 2012.

Shapiro, Nicholas. 2015. "Attuning to the Chemosphere: Domestic Formaldehyde, Bodily Reasoning, and the Chemical Sublime." *Cultural Anthropology* 30, no. 3 (2015): 368–93.

Shaw, Al, and Lylla Younes. "The Most Detailed Map of Cancer-Causing Industrial Air Pollution in the U.S." ProPublica, November 2, 2021; updated March 15, 2022. https://projects.propublica.org/toxmap/.

Slotta, James. "Revelations of the World: Transnationalism and the Politics of Perception in Papua New Guinea." *American Anthropologist* 116, no. 3 (2014): 626–42.

Sontag, Susan. *"Illness as Metaphor" and "AIDS and Its Metaphors."* New York: Picador, 2001.

Stengers, Isabelle. "History through the Middle: Between Macro and Mesopolitics." Interview by Brian Massumi and Erin Manning. *INFLeXions*, no. 3 (October 2009). http://www.inflexions.org/n3_History-through-the-Middle -Between-Macro-and-Mesopolitics-1.pdf.

Stengers, Isabelle. "Introductory Notes on an Ecology of Practices." *Cultural Studies Review* 11, no. 1 (2005): 183–96.

Stewart, Kathleen. "Atmospheric Attunements." *Environment and Planning D: Society and Space* 29, no. 3 (2011): 445–53.

Stewart, Kathleen. "On the Politics of Cultural Theory: A Case for 'Contaminated' Cultural Critique." *Social Research* 58, no. 2 (1991): 395–412.

Stewart, Kathleen. *Ordinary Affects*. Durham, NC: Duke University Press, 2007.

Stewart, Kathleen. "Regionality." *Geographical Review* 103, no. 2 (2013): 275–84.

Stewart, Kathleen. *A Space on the Side of the Road: Cultural Poetics in an "Other" America*. Princeton, NJ: Princeton University Press, 1996.

Stewart, Kathleen. "Studying Unformed Objects: The Provocation of a Compositional Mode." Member Voices, *Fieldsights*, June 30, 2013. https://culanth .org/fieldsights/350-studying-unformed-objects-the-provocation-of-a -compositional-mode.

Stewart, Kathleen. "Worlding Refrains." In *The Affect Theory Reader*, edited by Melissa Gregg and Gregory J. Seigworth, 339–53. Durham, NC: Duke University Press, 2010.

Tate, Shirley Anne. "Racial Affective Economies, Disalienation, and Race Made Ordinary." *Ethnic and Racial Studies* 37, no. 13 (2014): 2475–90.

Taylor, Charles. *Modern Social Imaginaries*. Durham, NC: Duke University Press, 2003.

Vance, J. D. *Hillbilly Elegy: A Memoir of a Family and Culture in Crisis*. New York: Harper, 2018.

Warner, Michael. "Tongues Untied: Memoirs of a Pentecostal Boyhood." In *Curiouser: On the Queerness of Children*, edited by Steven Bruhm and Natasha Hurley, 215–25. Minneapolis: University of Minnesota Press, 2004.

Williams, Raymond. *Marxism and Literature*. Oxford: Oxford University Press, 1978.

Wray, Matt. *Not Quite White: White Trash and the Boundaries of Whiteness*. Durham, NC: Duke University Press, 2006.

Wuthnow, Robert. *American Mythos: Why Our Best Efforts to Be a Better Nation Fall Short*. Princeton, NJ: Princeton University Press, 2008.

Index

(*see also* Gulf Oil; Texaco); refineries, 3, 28, 53. *See also* Big Oil

Old River, 2, 6

Orange, 2, 75

Page, Kathy, 30–31

people of color, 10, 44; rural, 97

Piney Woods, 23, 44, 52, 106, 111

poetics: of conservatism, 115; of petroculture, 27; of storytelling forms in SE Texas

Port Arthur, 2, 20, 24, 53, 95

QAnon, 12–13, 121n32

queer epiphany stories, 85–86, 88

queerness, 80, 83–86, 88–89

queer studies, 82; rural, 88

race, 10; stories of, 46

racism, 37, 45

real, the, 42–43, 69; of the queer world, 86

redemption, 25, 54; queer, 88

Refinery Belt, 27–28, 102–3

regionalism, 8, 65, 84, 88

religion, 10, 13, 22, 50, 56, 74; character and, 5. *See also* Catholic Church; Christianity; churches; fundamentalism; Islam

religiosity, 49, 75

rurality, 8, 19, 27, 33, 87; aestheticization of, 97; queer, 80

Schüll, Natasha Dow, 108, 110

secularism, 49, 56, 61

seepage, 102, 104, 106

severity, 14, 34, 40–42, 79, 117; affective states of, 77. *See also* suffering

sexuality, 10, 51–52

Shapiro, Nicholas, 99, 104

sociality, 11, 84, 90, 103, 111; normative, 15; queerness's function as, 85; Texan, 65. *See also* biosociality; Texan politesse

storytelling, 18, 26, 31, 52, 99; Texan, 4. *See also* abjection: comic

stuckness, 4, 9–10, 13, 23, 37

stuck relations, 22, 36, 81, 99

suffering, 10, 12, 22, 25, 40–41, 51; cancer and, 105; histories of, 99; mutual, 67; narratives of, 62

sundown towns, 9, 45

superstition, 68–69, 100

temporality, 22, 33–34, 109; of Benjamin's version of history, 9; of Hell, 54

Texaco, 28, 122n13

Texan politesse, 45, 65, 73, 111, 116, 123n16

Texas Oil Boom, 27–28, 84

Trinity River, 2, 77

Trump, Donald, 7, 9–13, 23, 97

Tyrrell, Michael, 59–60, 123n13

Vidor, 8–9, 12–13, 20, 25–26, 29–31, 34, 37, 44–46, 82, 120n23

violence: in SE Texas, 43; slow, 99

Western Atakapa, 6, 120n22

whenever ("punctual whenever"), 22–24, 122n7

whiteness, 7–8, 43, 45–46; rural, 10

white working class, 9, 11

wildcatters, 27–28

www.ingramcontent.com/pod-product-compliance
Lightning Source LLC
Chambersburg PA
CBHW050654270326
41927CB00012B/3026